Beyond the Resume

A Comprehensive Guide to Making the Right Impression Through E-mail, Cover Letters, Resumes, and Pre-Interviews

By Peter Gray and John Carroll

CAREER
PRESS

Franklin Lakes, NJ

BEYOND THE RESUME
EDITED AND TYPESET BY CHRISTOPHER CAROLEI
Cover design by The Visual Group
Printed in the U.S.A. by Book-mart Press

To order this title, please call toll-free 1-800-CAREER-1 (NJ and Canada: 201-848-0310) to order using VISA or MasterCard, or for further information on books from Career Press.

The Career Press, Inc., 3 Tice Road, PO Box 687,
Franklin Lakes, NJ 07417
www.careerpress.com

CAREER
PRESS

Library of Congress Cataloging-in-Publication Data

Gray, Peter.
    Beyond the resume: a comprehensive guide to making the right
impression through e-mail, cover letters, resumes, and pre-interviews/
by Peter Gray and John Carroll.
        p. cm.
    Includes index.
    ISBN-13: 978-1-56414-883-4
    ISBN-10: 1-56414-883-1 (paper)
1. Job hunting. 2. Interpersonal communication. I. Carroll, John. II.
    Title.

HF5382.7.G725 2006
650.14--dc22

                                                        2006043956

Acknowledgments

We want to thank the wonderful people at Career Press who made writing this book a true pleasure. We also want to thank Marilyn Allen, our literary agent, for her advice and direction. We particularly thank our wives, whose encouragement kept us focused on our writing process. We hope you, the readers, enjoy the results of our work and find the tips and phrases lead to your landing the job of your dreams.

Contents

Introduction

Thank you for choosing this book. We believe you will find it to be an excellent and unique resource when pursuing and interviewing for a new position. This book differs significantly from the others by virtue of transcending all phases of a job search: advanced tactics to developing a resume, writing letters, networking, cold calling companies and recruiters, leaving voice mail, steering a social conversation, managing the interview, responding to trick and nonrelevant questions, post-interview correspondence, and dealing with the four important types of communication styles, as well as intergenerational communications. The intent is to arm you with powerful and provoking phrases that catch the listener's or reader's interest and enable you to follow up with meaningful information, rather than just being glib or using buzzwords. One book covers all you need to know!

Our book goes beyond the resume and the classic job search and addresses unique tips and phrases for letters, telephone calls, voice mails, e-mails, and interviews that work in the real world and will get you hired. The advice, tips, materials, and phrases in the book will help arm you with appropriate actions to take. It is not the intent of the book to "prop you up" to sound as though you're something you are not. Instead, it is to aid in speaking about your strengths, experiences, and job know-how. This a "soup to nuts" kind of book and will show you what to do from the point of initial contact with the hiring authority, through interviewing, and on through closing the "deal." As a result, you will find this book to be of help to you if you are looking to advance to more responsible positions inside or outside your current place of employment, to change careers, or if you are an upcoming or recent graduate college looking for first-time employment, a military person seeking a civilian job, or a mature or retired individual seeking to return to the workforce.

Successfully landing a new job requires effective communications. You often have but one opportunity to get a person's attention and express who you are and what you are seeking. Consequently, the phrases you use to state your intentions and describe yourself are critical, and are what will make a difference between being acknowledged or being rejected. Consequently, we have chapters devoted to written communications via letter and e-mail, telephone calls and voice mails, networking, phrases specific to your industry and profession, and tips and phrases for unique situations relating to your experience level. A special feature in the book is the chapter on style and generational differences, which helps you adapt your communications to best fit your audience. We also address the common denominators in jobs and interviews, regardless of the industry and profession.

As you read through the phrases, keep in mind that the phrases we offer are simply examples. They are less intended as the exact phrase to use in a certain situation and meant more to provoke your own unique statements. Each chapter will cover a different scenario or set of circumstances where using the right phrases will pay off for the reader. Rationale will be discussed, do's and don'ts highlighted, and advice given on how to construct and use the phrases.

To help you create your own customized phrases, each chapter ends with an action planning or workbook segment where you can organize thoughts and develop personalized phrases. Use this section to anticipate questions, situations, or opportunities that might surface in your job search. By doing so, you gain a competitive edge over others who are pursuing the same job. Because you will learn to anticipate these issues, you will be prepared with well-thought-out answers. Once you have identified your phrases, take the time to rehearse them and outline the details that will support the statement. Read your notes at the end of each chapter before you begin to write a letter, send an e-mail, make a phone call, or go in for an interview. Practice your phrases and statements until you are comfortable saying them (yet do not sound glib or insincere).

For those who seek to learn more about resume writing and the job search process, there are several books we recommend. Two books on resumes are *Competency-Based Resumes* (Career Press, 2004), by Robin Kessler and Linda A. Strasberg, and *High-Level Resumes* (Career Press, 2005), by Marshall Brown and Annabelle Reitman. An outstanding resource for the job search process is Dr. Paul Powers's book, *Winning Job Interviews* (Career Press, 2004). Additionally, many other career-related books can be found at *www.careerpress.com*.

CHAPTER 1

Phrases That
Get the Word Out

What are the attention-getting phrases you use when making initial contact with individuals, interviewers, or people in general who are in a position to help you with your job search? When you are trying to get the word out about yourself, your work experiences, and your career interests, you basically are performing a marketing activity. The person you are reaching out to, in all likelihood, does not know you and, because the person is always busy, you must not waste anytime in introducing yourself. You have several objectives when "getting the word" out: to be quick, to be concise, and to have a compelling message so the person will want to learn more about you, remember you, and make a decision in your favor.

Basically your choices are calling, e-mailing, mailing, or making contact in person. What if you don't know how to reach the person—that is, you don't know his or her address, phone number, or e-mail? All is not lost as the Internet is a great resource for finding this information. By using any search engine you often can locate company Websites, telephone directories, or numbers (including cell numbers in some instances), e-mail addresses, biographies, association membership, quotes, and lots of other information that will help you reach the person and use powerful, persuasive phrases to get hired.

Cold-Calling Phrases

A telephone never feels any heavier than when you pick it up to call a stranger. Making a cold call to a recruiter, a company representative, the hiring manager or executive, or the gatekeeper to the person to whom you want to speak, is challenging. What do I say? What if I make a mistake? What if the person says no? What if the person says yes? We all have hesitations and excuses when it comes to making these calls. Yet, if you think about it, you have nothing to lose by making the call, and everything to gain if you are successful in getting the person to say yes. If we want the job then we must make the call. It all comes down to making that call.

Cold calling a hiring manager can be one of the best ways to gain employment. It is direct, is personal, and gives you the ability to gain information that might not be available through other sources. It also sets you apart from the crowd. Most people will simply mail, e-mail, or fax a resume. Although this can work, its effectiveness is increased severalfold when combined with a call to the appropriate person. You can improve the odds by making sure you use the right opening and closing phrases.

Your message should start by quickly introducing yourself: "My name is [name] and I am calling about [position]. I have significant experience in this area and would like to receive candidacy consideration. [Pause to hear what the individual says, which will tell you how to proceed]. What do you recommend I do?"

You may be fortunate to be asked questions about you background and accomplishments. Be prepared and respond with an overview of your key achievements and competencies. Ask the individual if that information helps, or if that is what he or she needs. If yes, ask for an appointment.

Again, the objective is to introduce yourself, gain a yes or no answer, and, if yes, a commitment to a next step. The next step could be as simple as calling back another time, or as encouraging as being invited in for an interview. Here are some phrases that help you get the word out via a telephone call to someone you do not know:

▶ "I am calling to introduce myself and to see if you are looking to expand your team. I am an experienced [cite profession and type of work done]."

▶ "I've heard that your firm may be looking for someone with my qualifications [quickly cite qualifications]."

▶ "I have recently become aware of your firm and thought we may have needs that coincide. [Wait for response or question.]"

▶ "I understand you have an opening for [cite position] and was hoping to understand where you are in your search, as I have worked in similar positions."

▶ "My name is [name] and I am calling about the [title] position that is open in your company. I am an experienced [profession] and wish to be considered."

▶ "Are you currently looking to hire in the area of [cite profession or skill]?"

▶ "Do you know of other areas in the company that might have a need for someone like me?"

▶ "I was given your name by [name] in our company, who recommended that I give you a call regarding your [title] opportunity."

▸ "I recently read an article about your firm and was interested to see if you are looking to hire [profession]."

▸ "I currently work as a [title] for [name] company and wanted to see if you utilize talent in that area."

Warming Up a Cold Call

People connect for many reasons. By nature, people need social, physical, intellectual, and aesthetic outlets. If you can find commonalities between you and the person you are calling (before you make the call) he or she will almost always be more receptive. These commonalities can be anything. It can be the town you live in. Mentioning that you two are "neighbors" humanizes you and makes it much harder for the person on the other end to "get you off the phone." It also makes him or her want to help. Because you are part of the same community, and people want to be well thought of and liked within their community, it raises the stakes for them. Other areas you might find commonalities can include: your religious organization, a playhouse, symphony, or center for the arts you are involved in or attend, charities you participate in, volunteer organizations, communal activities, sports club, wine clubs, culinary groups, cooking classes, and so on. Most of these groups have publications of some kind. Take a look. See who the donors are. Also take notice of who is involved with what in the notes of recognition in the publications. If there is no publication, talk around. You'll be very likely to find out that there are some central people who are very passionately involved in one way or another in the group. Also, make sure that everyone you run into within the group knows that you are skilled and looking for a new opportunity.

Networking Phrases

One of the best ways to get the word out about you is to constantly network. Every person you know in your work and personal life is a potential networking contact. The same goes for people you meet for the first time on an airplane, on the street, at a conference, during a social event, at your child's school program, waiting in line at the dry cleaners, at a neighborhood block party, and the possibilities go on and on. Every time you are in front of someone, or every time you are on the phone with someone, it is an opportunity to network. Networking is marketing *you*—what you do, who you are, and what you can do for others. Marketing yourself involves describing yourself so that the person wants to know more about you, and walks away with a lasting memory of who you are and what you do. In some instances it is marketing yourself so that what you do is what the other person needs.

Because you may have only a couple of sentences to capture the attention of someone you meet you must make sure that the introduction of each other is informative. Networking is more than just sharing names, titles, employers, and each other's business cards (make sure you do get a card to record notes and to get a telephone number). Networking is presenting yourself in a way that that the other person will recognize a personal need for what you do, know of others who need what you do or have, and remember you in future times should someone ask the individual if he or she knows someone who does *x*, *y*, and *z*.

When meeting someone for the first time in a business, social, or networking situation, you should immediately introduce yourself and ask the person who he or she is, and what he or she does. So, for example, you might say, "Hello, my name is Fred Smith. And you are?" Then ask the person what he or she does, or why he or she is at that event. Inevitably the person will ask you what you do. You have only one chance to make a memorable and positive impression. You want to tailor your networking introduction, as much as possible, to the person's own station in life and work.

Don't diminish it by stating your title and the company for whom you work. That tells the person very little and leaves one unimpressed. When someone states that he or she is an accountant, a sales manager, a production supervisor, a marketing VP, or what ever the title, what does it say about the person? Does it convey what one does? What you can do for them? Of course not! Accountants, for example, are a dime a dozen, but someone who "helps companies leverage their returns on their assets" is something different. See the difference? Stating one's title leaves people in the dark, but defining the outcome of what you do hits home.

You want to use phrases in your introduction that make you stand out from others in your job, profession, or company. Here are some phrases to model or modify for your use in networking introductions. Where possible, one's phrase should not only describe what one does, but what outcome results from it:

▸ "I work with individuals who seek to improve their financial holdings and be set for retirement." [financial planner]

▸ "I help individuals set and achieve personal and work goals." [personal or business coach]

▸ "I help companies source and retain talent in order to grow their business." [recruiter]

▸ "I work with individuals and organizations that want to unclutter their work and be more efficient." [personal or business organizer]

▸ "I help companies improve their customer image and gain more repeat business." [customer-service professional, order-entry person]

▸ "Companies who want to maximize their return on assets and minimize their cash flow need me." [finance professional, asset accountant, CFO]

▸ "I help nonprofit organizations identify their true mission, clarify goals, and develop action plans to achieve them." [strategic planning professional]

▸ "Companies who want to leverage and reward sales performance need my skills." [sales trainer, sales-compensation expert]

▸ "I help organizations come together as a team and use this power to achieve unimagined results." [team-building expert, human resources trainer]

▸ "Individuals who seek to make better presentations and win over their audiences benefit from my programs." [public-speaking coach]

▸ "I help companies perfect their production processes, achieve high levels of efficiency and quality, and lower their costs." [industrial engineer, quality engineer]

See how powerful phrases such as these can be? They prompt responses such as, "Tell me more," "How exactly do you do that?", "Where do you do this?", "How did you get into the field?", and so on. Now you are in control of the conversation. You can tell more about who you are, what you do, the results that come from your work, and much more. You now have license to ask the person some questions such as:

▸ "Does your company have a need for people like me?"

▸ "Do you know of someone who can benefit from my experience and accomplishments?"

▸ "Can you suggest some companies that are looking for talent like me?"

▸ "Is there something I can do for you?"

▸ "How did you get into this field/company? Is that a possibility for me?"

▸ "I admire your success and would like to emulate it. Do you have any recommendations?"

▶ "Are there some good books you can recommend that I read to give myself a better chance in your industry/firm?"

Now that you see that networking can be quite powerful when you use the right phrases, start thinking about where people network or congregate. Where do the individual(s) you seek to contact work or socialize? What associations and local chapter meetings might they belong to and attend? What conferences or trade shows center around the people you wish to meet? Community organizations? Perhaps you should be in attendance, too, armed with your networking phrases and introductions.

Keep the Network Going

Just because you have not found a job through one particular person it is no reason to cut him or her off from your network. Similarly, if you have been "rejected" by a firm, *keep it in your network*. These individuals still have valuable contacts, and new openings do come up from time to time. I have often seen a candidate go in to interview with a hiring manager and get "rejected" for the job, only to be called back weeks or even months later and get an offer for a different job. One way to keep these people in your network is to keep them informed about the status of your job hunt. Tell them about the companies you have met with, or are meeting with. Let them know when you have started a new position. By doing so, you will maintain a valuable resource for your next job search.

If you fail to call these people until you are looking again, perhaps years later, you will have lost most of the benefit of your network. Part of maintaining an active network is keeping in touch. This kind of network grooming has additional benefits. As the people in your network move up or change direction, you will gain more opportunities. Neglecting to maintain a network is a sin, especially because it is so easy to keep up with it. Here are few easy and painless ways to maintain your network:

▸ Send relevant news clippings and articles.

▸ Occasionally e-mail contacts with exciting industry news, and ask how they are doing.

▸ Send a letter (a thank you, an update, a change of address).

▸ Offer them minor-league tickets, movie tickets, or other goodies.

▸ Let them know about an upcoming community event.

▸ Ask them if they want to participate by donating to a charity you are involved with.

▸ Invite them to lunch.

Warm-Call Phone Phrases

Not all telephone calls are cold calls as previously described. Often you are putting in a call to people you have previously dealt with in the company you are targeting for employment, or to personal acquaintances or business contacts. People who know you are more apt to take or return your call. They are also individuals who are more likely to help you with your job search. Don't wear out your welcome by being long-winded. Similarly as you do with a cold call, state the purpose of the call and ask if they will help you.

Want to know a secret on how to turn a cold call into a warm call? As previously mentioned (and well worth repeating), share something the two of you have in common. It could be a mutual acquaintance, a hobby or sport, an association membership, a place of worship, a common city of residence, or perhaps you heard the person speak at a meeting. It takes a little effort, such as doing a Web search, but you can find information about the person that turns the call from cold to warm! Here are some examples:

- ▶ "It's been a long time since we have talked."
- ▶ "I am hoping to make a career change."
- ▶ "What areas do you think are hot right now?"
- ▶ "Which companies have you seen experience explosive growth?"
- ▶ "If you were searching for a job, which companies do you think you might go after?"
- ▶ "You remember me from [situation], and I wanted to get your opinion on [topic]."
- ▶ "How are things going in your industry?"
- ▶ "What kind of needs are there in your firm?"
- ▶ "Will you take a look at my resume and make suggestions?"
- ▶ "What do you think I can do to leverage my experience?"
- ▶ "Are there any additional skills I should learn to increase my value to a prospective employer?"
- ▶ "Can you tell me what areas your company is hiring in?"
- ▶ "Whom should I contact in your company to learn about position openings, and can I use your name?"
- ▶ "I learned that your company has an opening for [title]. Any suggestions as to how I might go about applying? Do you know the manager in this department?"

E-mail Phrases

The technology of e-mail has totally changed how we communicate with one another. It allows us to reach people 24 hours a day, seven days a week, and it encourages a response because it is easy to do so. Unlike regular printed mail, e-mail may not be screened by a secretary or administrative assistant. It, however, can be deleted or filtered out in a nanosecond should the subject line not be of interest to the recipient or the sender's address is blocked.

Remember that your e-mail may be one of dozens, even hundreds that the individual receives daily. So it must stand out from the others. You do this not by marking the e-mail *urgent*, but by making the subject line jump out. This is achieved by: (1) quoting from document(s) about the position [the job description, recruitment advertisement, earlier conversation, and so on], (2) referencing the name of a mutually known individual, or (3) using creative, hard-hitting, attention-getting phrases.

Furthermore, after getting the person's attention (in other words, making him or her want to read your e-mail), you must quickly state why you are e-mailing, why you are a fit for the job, and what you intend to do next or expect from the person. Lastly, if you are expecting your resume to help you sell yourself, good luck! If it is appended to the e-mail as an attachment it may never be opened because the person: (a) has no interest in seeing it, (b) doesn't have the time to open, view, or print the document, (c) cannot open the document file format, or (d) has concerns about viruses in an attachment (from a stranger).

Critics are divided as to whether or not to include your resume with your e-mail. Some people recommend you quickly summarize who you are and highlight, in the e-mail, your key accomplishments, background, and interests in this company or position. That is all. It becomes an introduction and a very positive one at that. Should it pique the reader's interest, he or she, for certain, will get back to you with a request for your resume.

If you feel it important to include your resume, it is better to paste a text version (.txt, .rft, and so on) of the resume right after the e-mail message than it is to have a separate attachment. This way there is no chance that the resume will be accidentally separated from the e-mail when printed. Don't be concerned about the recipient not having a *neat, clean, digital copy of your resume*. If he or she is impressed with the e-mail, he or she will seek you out for a clean copy, or to talk.

The subject line of an e-mail is often all one sees when making a decision to open and read the e-mail. It is your *door opener,* so make it succinct, to the point, and meaningful. Here are some sample e-mail phrases for the heading of the e-mail:

- ▸ "Regarding [name of position]—can you lead me in the right direction?" (For example, "Regarding the Senior Accountant position opening, can you lead me in the right direction?")
- ▸ "Appreciate candidacy consideration for the position of [position title]."
- ▸ "Skilled [name profession]. Very interested in your position opening of [job title]." (For example, "Accomplished public relations professional. Very interested in your position of Media Specialist.")
- ▸ "[Your company name] [position title] seeks to advance." (If your company has immediate name recognition and respect then, by all means, use it. For example, "Proctor and Gamble Marketing Analyst seeks new career opportunities.")
- ▸ "[Name of mutual contact] suggested I write."
- ▸ "Job openings? I am interested in your company."
- ▸ "[Industry] expert seeking employment."

In the body of the e-mail launch your introduction by using a phrase different from that used in the heading of the e-mail. Continue with key accomplishments and important background information. As always, end with an action step: "I will call you tomorrow," "Please advise regarding your interest," "Work samples available. Would you like to see?", "I will be in the area of your offices tomorrow afternoon and would like to schedule a time to meet."

Voice-Mail Phrases

One of the best vehicles for getting your name out in front of someone is by voice mail. Many people prefer voice mail to having someone answer the phone. Why? Because with voice mail you have no interruptions or questions from the other end of the line. You can (and should!) script your voice-mail message before you dial the number. Practice it so it doesn't sound as if you are reading it off a piece of paper. Keep it short and to the point. Remember that you can always press the button (usually the # button) to erase and rerecord (something you cannot do when talking live!).

Always be prepared for someone to answer the phone. If you get voice mail directly, great. Leave your scripted message. If you get a "gatekeeper" (a secretary, assistant, or receptionist), you have to decide whether to leave a live message or ask to be transferred to the person's voice mail. If you need to talk to the person immediately and are asking for a prompt call back, then leave a live message with the person who answers the phone. That way you can verbally (words and tone) leave a message that conveys urgency. The person may feel compelled to walk in the message or alert the manager as soon as he or she is free. Urgent messages should not be left, initially, for voice mail, as the person may not immediately check messages. Try to connect with a human and leave your important message. If you don't hear back shortly, then call and leave a follow-up message.

Otherwise, if it is not a pressing message, opt for voice mail. The person will ultimately check it. Similarly, if you want to increase the odds of getting a person's voice mail, call before or after hours, on the weekend, or at lunchtime. You, of course, will need the person's direct-dial number or extension for automated systems.

Your objectives with your voice-mail message are four-fold. First, you need to identify yourself and how you can be reached. Second, you must state why you are calling. Third, you need to leave a tight, to-the-point statement of why you are calling (don't forget that your networking introduction might be appropriate!). Finally, you should convey an active, not passive, statement about what you expect, what you want the person to do, or what you intend to do. The last item is very important as it commits the recipient of the message to do something or expect something, rather than ignore and erase the message. It forces the person to evaluate the message, make a decision, and communicate that decision by calling you back or preparing for your next call.

Again, remember there has to be a way for the recipient to contact you, and there should be a specific action requested at the end of the message, so it is generally beneficial to leave your contact information at both the beginning and the end of the message. This way, if one part is unclear, hopefully, the other one will be intelligible. Also, should the message need to be replayed, the recipient will not have to listen to the entire message again just the get your telephone number. Here are some phrases you can use:

▶ "I'm calling to introduce myself as a skilled [profession]. If you have need for someone with my skills, please call me back at [number]."

▶ "I understand you are looking for a [profession]. Please call me to discuss...."

▶ "I got your name from [name]. Please call me when you get a chance."

▶ "I am calling to discuss your [profession] needs."

▶ "Hi, this is [your name and number]. Please call me when you get a chance. Again, this is [your name and number]."

▶ "I was hoping you might be able to direct me to the person in change of hiring. My number is [your number]."

▸ "If you need assistance in [your skills], please call me at [your number]."

▸ "I am a licensed [your profession] who is currently seeking employment."

▸ "If you are shorthanded in the [your skills] department, I can help out. My number is [your number]."

▸ "Please call me if your division needs a skilled [your profession]. Again, I am at [your number]."

Phrases for the "Message-Taker"

Often, someone other than the person you are trying to reach will answer the phone. Should a secretary, executive or administrative assistant, receptionist, or someone else answer the phone, the voice-mail script, with slight modification, is ideal. The person will either put you through or ask to take a message and, of course, you already know what to say.

In some respects, leaving a message this way offers a bonus. You have the opportunity to ask questions, probe, and receive important information. For example:

▸ "When do you expect her to return?"

▸ "What is the best time to call back?"

▸ "Can you tell me if the position has been filled?"

▸ "Is she conducting interviews?"

▸ "Does he already have enough candidates?"

▸ "At what stage is your boss in the search and interview process?"

▸ "Is this job search being handled through a search agency or recruiter? Who might that be?"

▸ "Knowing that I have [blank] experience, would you recommend I talk with her?" (You may learn what else is important).

▸ "Could he call me at [time]?", "Can I call back at [time]?", "What time do you suggest is best for me to call again?" (The questions force one to say yes/no, or suggest an alternative time).

▸ "[Name] said I should call. Do you know this person?" (This enables you to learn if the person is highly regarded).

Follow-Up Phrases (After the Initial Contact)

So you were successful in writing or reaching the person via one of the previously mentioned modes. What about your follow-up communication? Whether or not you have heard back from the person, you must take the initiative to follow up, even if for no other reason than to thank the person. As with your first contact effort, you may be restricted to the same mode of communication, or you may have new options. For example, you now may have a direct-dial number or e-mail address, or know the secretary by first name. Decide which mode is most appropriate for you to send any follow-up communications and say:

▸ "I am calling to see what the next step is."

▸ "I am calling to see if you need more information. As you may have noticed from my resume I have [cite experience]."

▸ "Thank you so much for talking with me, where do we go from here?"

▸ "It was a pleasure talking with you. I hope to get the opportunity to work in your division. When might I be hearing from you?"

▸ "Has there been any change in status for the position we discussed?"

▸ "Do you think a second meeting is appropriate at this time?"

▸ "How did you feel about my credentials?"

▸ "Do you feel that I would make a strong candidate for the position we discussed?"

▸ "Thank you so much for the lead. It was a real pleasure meeting you yesterday."

▸ "I really appreciate all your advice. I'll certainly keep you in the loop."

▸ "I really appreciate any leads you might be able to offer."

▸ "Do you know of any industry trade shows that might give me some exposure?"

▸ "I am calling to see where we are in the interview process."

▸ "I am calling to follow up as we discussed."

▸ "I have new information I would like to share with you."

▸ "There are a few issues that I wanted to discuss with you."

Chapter Worksheet

As a result of the previous information, what is your communication strategy going forward? What phrases do you need to develop and perfect to *get the word out*?

Describe the job for which you are applying:

▸ Describe the company that has the job opening.

▸ What are the skills, talents, strengths you want to stress?

▸ How do you plan to communicate to the company and/or individual?

What phrases are a fit for you when:

▸ Cold calling?

▸ Warm calling?

▶ Making a networking introduction?
▶ Leaving a voice mail?
▶ Leaving a message with someone?
▶ Sending an e-mail?
▶ Writing a letter?
▶ Following up?

What will you do to warm up your cold calls?

CHAPTER 2

Cover Letter and
Resume Phrases

Similar to the expression "it takes two to tango," your cover letter and resume are two distinctly different, yet inseparable, documents. Each must stand on its own, and, in tandem, are powerful papers that describe you, your skills and accomplishments, your knowledge and competencies, and why you are the right person for the position. It goes without saying that both must be crisply crafted and be nothing less than exceptional. Your hopes of getting the reader's complete attention and of taking your candidacy to the next step can be dashed, however, if the letter or resume, or both, are poorly composed.

A poorly written letter can prompt a recruiter, human resources official, or the hiring manager to skip reading the resume. Similarly, a poorly presented resume can create negative images despite its containing important content. Although it is substance, rather than first impressions, that ultimately clinches an offer, the latter is what prompts the reader to take positive action. That action can take many forms, including:

putting the letter and resume in a pile for reading later, jotting notes in the margin, forwarding it to the hiring manager, or calling you. So, given the importance and linkage of these two documents let's take a closer look at the purpose and content of the cover letter and the resume.

The Cover Letter

The cover letter is how you introduce yourself and state your intent. People's intentions are often diverse when writing a letter. Are you educating the reader? Are you reaching out in a general way to inform the reader of your background and job interests? Are you asking for networking help? Are you writing in response to a specific position advertisement, or out of knowledge of a job opening in the company? Regardless of the objective, all of your letters must contain phrases that relay: (1) your expectations of the person (often requesting consideration for a position), (2) what makes that expectation realistic (your qualifications), and (3) how the individual might reach you and what you intend to do if you aren't contacted.

Networking Letters

This type of communication should be short but personal, and motivate the recipient to want to help you with your job search or request. Your friends and business contacts may not know details about your work and profession, so you need to briefly share these with them. Then, after introducing your situation, you need to quickly summarize what you do and what typical positions and titles apply to you.

> You and I worked together on the Band Boosters committee. I am writing you to ask for your help with my job search. My position as an accountant was one of many jobs eliminated at Alpha Corporation as a result of a downturn in the after-market parts business. Positions such as

financial analyst, accounting supervisor, or general led-
ger accounting are typically ones for which I qualify.
Should you learn of such an opening at your place of
work would you mind sharing this resume with the HR
department or the hiring manager? Many thanks. I can be
reached at 555-555-1212 should you have any questions. I
will call you in a week to fill you in on my search.

Remember that you need to be very specific about what
you want him or her to do as a result of your resume submis-
sion. It is human nature to want to help someone, but people
want to know exactly what they can do. It isn't good enough to
say, "Let me know if you hear of anything." Be very specific
(for example, "I would appreciate it if you would share my
resume with your company's market-research manager," or
"Do you know Bill Schmidt in your production planning department? If you do, would you mind passing on my resume?").

Don't be bashful! By being bold with your request you
have a higher probability of success. It helps clarify what the
person can realistically do—if he or she can't, he will certainly
tell you. Lastly, remember that this is a networking letter, so
don't forget to put in writing one of your verbal networking
phases to help the individual make the connection between
you and what you do.

General Letters of Introduction

These letters may be part of your job search strategy, but
keep in mind that companies and recruiters receive hundreds
of letters each day inquiring about job opportunities and asking for consideration for any "appropriate" positions that may
be open currently or in the future. (Do not send a letter
[through standard mail] if the company uses an online resume/
application system as the preferred method of making known
your availability and interest.) The longer the letter the less
likely it will be read. Help the reader out by putting a topic in
bold at the upper right hand portion of the page. Be brief, use

phrases that describe you in a broad way, and let your resume deal with specific accomplishment phrases. The reader can best grasp who you are and what you do by simply knowing your current (or past) title, company, and salary. Make sure you reference a few details, and include buzz words where legitimate.

Chuck Smith
123 Main Street
Anytown, USA 12345

[Current Date]

Bill Johnson, Partner
Johnson and Jones Executive Recruiters
1010 High Street
Big City, USA 54321

RE: PRODUCTION SUPERINTENDENT SEEKS NEW CHALLENGES

Dear Mr. Johnson,

I write to alert you to my interest in taking on expanded responsibilities as a director or vice president of manufacturing. Regarded as a strong developer of people and builder of teams, I am currently overseeing a three-shift, lean manufacturing-based tooling and machining operation employing 400 people. By instituting six-sigma process improvement techniques I have reduced throughput times by 35 percent and these efficiencies have resulted in a 50 percent reduction in operating costs. Consequently, ABC Company has gained in market share and returned to profitability.

I would appreciate candidacy consideration for any related client search currently underway or planned. My current base salary is $145,000 plus a bonus. I can be reached at 999-244-2424 days, or 999-454-5454 evenings.

Sincerely,

Chuck Smith

Why the simplicity? So as to increase the probability that the letter will stand out and will be read! Don't put barriers in the way of someone's limited time by writing a lengthy tome about yourself. This will give the recipient a reason not to read the letter. Your objective is to capture his or her attention and get him to act on the letter and resume, even if it is only to be filed (versus thrown away) or scanned into a searchable resume database for future reference (which really was your objective to begin with).

Letters of Application for a Specific Position

Writing a letter for a specific position requires more thought and strategic positioning of phrases that will not only grab the reader's attention, but also summarize who you are, what you have accomplished, and why you are right for the job opening. Reference the position for which you are applying, highlight your current position and employer, and provide three to five key accomplishments of your career. When articulating your accomplishments, frame them so that you state the challenge or opportunity that faced you, the analysis or action you took to address the situation or problem, and, finally, the end result (quantify it in terms of time, output, percentages, monetary amounts, and so on). Don't go overboard, as you want to keep the length of your letter to one page. Make sure that the action statements do not replicate everything that is stated in your resume, but rather have them complement your resume. How might these statements look? Here are some examples:

▸ "Addressed unacceptable operating efficiencies by implementing just-in-time inventory practices with vendors. Overall production efficiencies grew from 82 percent to 97 percent."

▸ "Company facing stagnant market share. Grew market share by 10 points with an aggressive direct-mail advertising campaign."

▸ "Faced with short-term, negative-cash-flow situation implemented aggressive customer collections calling campaign and factoring of all new receivables. Resulted in a reduction of receivable days outstanding from 110 days to 54 days, and influx of $2.2 million dollars."

▸ "Faced with rising labor costs and inefficiencies, negotiated five-year labor contract with incentives for productivity improvements and reduction in number of job classifications from 55 to 13."

▸ "In an effort to secure improved product margins reduced number of models in product lines by 40 percent and introduced common-parts schemes. Resulted in 18 percent improvement in margins."

Next, allot a sentence or two to describing yourself, your values, and styles. Important tip: Take the time to review the help-wanted advertisement, job description, and company Website to ascertain what really is important to this company. Cite those accomplishments and personal traits that are most relevant. Do not repeat what is on your resume but, instead, make it a prelude to it. Cite a noteworthy achievement that will require the reader to go on to your resume. (For example, if the ad mentioning working in a *fast-paced* work environment, you might state, "In my resume you will see additional examples of time sensitive accomplishments.")

Unlike a general letter of introduction (where you relay just your current salary), also include your salary expectations for this opening. Some people think that this might rule you out for a job, but it is really the reverse: It *rules you in* by identifying your worth. Be broad and generous with your range. Obviously you are not interested in working for less than the low end of your range, and the hiring authority will now know your desires. Don't feel that by putting an upper limit to your expectations that you will "sell yourself short" if an offer ultimately comes through.

Finally, tell the reader when you intend to follow up, and how he or she can reach you in the interim:

> "I will call you next Wednesday to answer any questions you might have and to find out what the next step is in the pursuit of this opening. Should you want to reach me before then, I can be reached days at 999-666-3333, or by e-mail. Thank you, in advance, for your considerations."

Do not hesitate to highlight several key phrases or words in bold in order to draw one's attention to the most important part of you letter. If you have done your research, you will know the "drivers" for this job. If you have them in your background, make sure you point them out. Remember that everything is focused on getting the reader to take a *call to action* and move to the next step. The letter should prompt one to look at your resume, the resume should motivate the person to pick up the phone and call (or e-mail) you, your demeanor during the telephone call should result in an on-site interview, and so on.

Using Computer-Stored Letters and E-mail

The computer is a real time-saver when it comes to composing new letters and e-mails. Most of us recycle previously written documents. And why not? They are well-written documents that can serve new situations. The word of caution is that when you "cut and paste" the document make sure you do a word/phrase search to extract names, phrases, terms, and so on, that were germane to the previous recipient but not to the new one. Nothing is worse than receiving a letter where, for example, the salutation refers to someone else's name. The reader instantly knows that you did not craft the communication specifically for him or her or the company. The same applies with spelling and grammar check. Big words are great, but only if you spell them correctly (*entraprenerial* when you meant *entrepreneurial*!). Make sure the spelling is correct, and also make sure that you are using the right words where several spellings can exist (*principal* versus *principle*, *to* versus *too*, and so on), as these will not be caught by spell check. Remember to read the letter thoroughly to catch things that slip by spell check (*you* instead of *your*).

Handwritten Notes in a Letter

Do you know the person to whom you are writing? If so, a neatly handwritten letter is certainly in order. The better you know the person, the more personal the note or request can be. Even if you don't know the individual, a short note may be in order. Why? Go back to the concept of successive steps. Your objective is to get the recipient to read the letter. Often there is a gatekeeper involved, such as an administrative assistant, secretary, or designated person who is charged with screening the letters. If this gatekeeper believes you an important person in the boss's network, he or she will be more apt to let that letter and resume go through. Here are some examples:

▸ "We met last year at the CBA conference, where you suggested I contact you should I ever be interested in making a career move."

▸ "With my six-sigma black belt I can make a real difference with your client's operations."

▸ "Thank you for taking the time to review my resume. I know you will see a solid fit with the position specs."

▸ "I am looking forward to your call. You won't be disappointed."

▸ "I know the advertisement specified "local candidates" only, but given my strong credentials and very limited relocation expense (rent), I would appreciate special consideration."

- ▸ "Joyce Reynolds sends her regards."
- ▸ "I heard you speak at the Chamber's economic-outlook breakfast meeting."

The note makes it personal and serves as a bridge to the resume. Be brief, be neat, and be real! Where the letter is in response to a general address, do some research on the company and find out what you have in common, or what appeals to you about working there. Make that your "personal" note. Most importantly, never claim that you have met when you haven't. We experienced a situation where the recipient of the letter challenged the writer's claim to know him personally. Obviously you will not be considered by that person for any job!

The Resume

The word *resume* comes from the French etymology, *résumé,* which is the past participle of *résumer* (to summarize). Although most resumes are little more than a summary, yours should be different. Although some of the information will summarize your work experience, related skills, and education, focus on giving evidence that you have the capabilities to do the specific job you are applying for. If there happens to be a job description, you really are in luck. The bullets you provide should make it clear that you have the skills and experience they require as per the job description. If you do not meet all their criteria, don't rule yourself out. A candidate who has four out of five of the requirements may be very qualified, and in fact, there may be very little additional training needed.

Your resume is, in a way, your marketing tool. Keep this in mind throughout the resume-writing process. Emphasize what will be relevant and important to the employer, don't just list duties you have performed in the past. Many of them may be obvious. Talk about results. It's more impressive to say that you increased revenue by 140 percent than to just say that you made sales calls in your territory.

To that end, quantify when you can. People like numbers and hard facts. If hard figures are not readily available, use a good, yet conservative estimate. When you are in the interview, if you are asked about the number, it is completely acceptable to let the interviewer know that these numbers were the very best and most accurate estimate possible due to your situation. Make sure to tell them that these are conservative estimates, and that the actual figures are higher.

Also consider adding features and benefits. A feature is a trait or characteristic (such as, *used consultative approach*), whereas a benefit shows the employer what value the feature added (such as, *this resulted in a 30 percent increase in gross sales*).

Getting Visibility

This is your ultimate objective, and the resume can open or close doors for you—if it is read. Today it is difficult to get your resume read or reviewed. Companies and recruiters receive volumes of resumes in response to their ads. Retained search firms, when the word gets out about a confidential search, are flooded with mail. Very large firms may specify that all applications must be done online, as they have gone "paperless." Only in small firms will you find someone reviewing every resume.

Many companies save digital resumes, or use optical recognition scanning to capture your resume. If they do, it is possible that a human being may not look at your resume unless it surfaces in a search of key words and phrases. The same applies for applying online. Your profile now is part of a larger, searchable candidate database. This brings us back to the importance of having the right phrases and critical words in your resume. It is not the intent of this book to focus on how to write a resume. There are numerous books and resources available to master that. Instead, we would like to turbo-charge your resume by focusing on powerful, attention-grabbing words and phrases to use, regardless of whether your resume is organized chronologically or functionally.

Before you develop your words and phrases, ask yourself some important questions. What are the key words/phrases in your discipline, profession, and industry? What do you know about the company and what it seeks? What does the advertisement say? What does the online job description contain?

In this age of digital documents and letter-quality office or home printers there is no reason why you should not, just as you do with your cover letter, tailor your resume to the situation. Just make sure you keep track of the changes and modifications (and label it properly when filing it on your PC hard drive). Always do word searches to make sure you cleansed the resume (or cover letter) of unwanted words, phrases, or names. Nothing knocks you out of the running faster than a spelling error or poor grammar. When you go in for an interview make certain you bring along quality printed copies, and make certain they are the same as what you initially submitted. The same advice applies when you place a resume on a job board. Have more than one, if necessary, and update it periodically. The following are ideas about what key words or phrases to be included as part of your resume. Companies and recruiters often look for:

Degrees
▶ M.B.A.
▶ Ph.D.
▶ M.S.W.
▶ M.P.H.
▶ Chem. Engrg.
▶ M.D.
▶ Ed.D.
▶ Masters in Taxation
▶ J.D.

- B.A., B.S., B.A.S., or B.F.A.
- Psy. D.
- B.S.N.
- M.S.N.
- R.N.
- A.A., A.S., or A.A.S.
- M.A.T.
- D.M.D. or D.D.S.
- D.C. or D.C.M.
- D.B.A.

Certifications or Licenses

- CPA (certified public accountant)
- CEBS (certified employee benefit specialist)
- CMA (comparative marketing analysis, or certified management accountant)
- SPHR (senior professional in human rsources)
- PHR (professional in human resources)
- LPN (licensed practical nurse)
- LPCMH (licensed professional counselor of mental health)
- PMP (project management professional)
- CRI (Crown Research Institute)
- LCSW (licensed clinical social worker)
- CMP (cooperative marketing partner)
- MFT (marriage and family therapist)
- Series 7
- CPC (certified public coder)
- State-issued licenses (architect, plumber, realtor, and so on)

Societies, Associations, and Unions

- International Association of Management Consultants

- Society for Human Resource Management
- American Actuarial Association
- Electrochemical Society
- American Heart Association
- Industrial Hygiene Association
- National Notary Association
- American Bar Association
- American Marketing Association
- International Union of Electrical Workers
- National Education Association
- ASFME (Association of State, Federal, and Municipal Employees)

Quality or Process Improvement or Production Terms

- Lean manufacturing
- Six Sigma
- TQM (total quality management)
- Cell Names for Methodologies
- Just-in-time inventory control
- Manufacturing cells
- ISO 9000 Certified

Technical Jargon

- Polymers
- Database Management
- Java
- Process reengineering
- Change management
- Strategic planning
- Data Mining
- Cold Fusion
- MRP (manufacturing resources planning)
- Pivot Tables

- SQL (structured query language)
- eBusiness or eMarketing

The "C" Level Descriptors
- Chairman—Chairman of the Board
- CEO—Chief Executive Officer
- COO—Chief Operating Officer
- CFO—Chief Financial Officer
- CIO—Chief Information Officer
- CMO—Chief Marketing Officer
- CHRO—Chief Human Resources Officer
- CPO—Chief Personnel Officer
- General Counsel

Personal Descriptors and Titles
- Leadership
- Teambuilding
- Project Management
- Executive
- General Manager
- Assistant Vice President
- Superintendent
- Vice President
- Safety Officer
- Incident Commander
- Chairman
- Team Leader
- Production Coordinator
- Logistics Coordinator

Your objective is to have your resume surface ahead of others by virtue of having more hits with the anticipated key-word and phrase searches. Indeed, some search tools sort the results by order of strength or relevance. Some actually highlight in bold or in color the actual instances where the word or phrase is used. Naturally, the more frequent the occurrence the more positive the assumptions that are made regarding the individual.

"When you have it, flaunt it" is the advice about key words and phrases. However, never make yourself out to be something that isn't true. False statements about your background, employment, and accomplishments, and so on, will come out in an interview, or during a reference check, degree-verification call, and general inquiries. There is nothing improper, however, in using key terms with a qualifying descriptor attached:

- ▸ "Completed all coursework requirements for Ph.D. Only thesis remaining."
- ▸ "Currently a first-year student in two-year M.B.A. program."
- ▸ "Sitting for CPA exam first of next year."
- ▸ "Past member of SHRM."
- ▸ "Enrolled in six-sigma class at local community college."

Thus, while you are being very straightforward with your status, you have embedded important search words in your resume (enhancing the probability of your resume surfacing). You are hoping that the reader will not let your *almost am* statement(s) prejudice him or her, and that your accomplishments will make up for it. Many a person is hired despite not meeting all the candidate specs! Your goal is to make sure your resume does rise to the top and let the reader decide if you are of merit, despite not having all the requirements. Without the previous allusions, your resume might not be viewed at all. With them, at least it initially rises to someone's attention, and your other strengths and accomplishments may outweigh everything else.

Where you legitimately can claim ownership of a key word or phrase, make sure that you expand upon it by citing real circumstances and results. Now you are not a name dropper, as is the case with other resumes. Rather, you are demonstrating how you applied the knowledge associated with the term. For example:

▸ "Faced with rising in-process inventories, implemented cell- and lean-manufacturing techniques. Work-in-process material value reduced by $800,000 in three months."

▸ "Part of a task force comprised of Six-Sigma black belt holders. Chartered with identifying and implementing process breakthroughs that decreased FDA documentation and trial times by 60 percent."

▸ "Applied Website optimization principals to existing company site which increased click-down's by 30 percent."

▸ "Eliminated order-processing errors by applying Kepner-Tregoe problem-solving tools."

▸ "Coauthored financial book on private equity markets."

▸ "Developed all training curriculum in accordance with ADDIE principles."

▸ "Expanded Website to include streaming video for all product demonstrations."

It is appropriate here to also talk about things to avoid when developing key words and phrases. First, be real! Don't present yourself as having done something when you haven't. Don't exaggerate or stretch the truth. The second word of caution is with the use of cliches and often-used adjectives such as *team-player, results-oriented, multitasking, hands-on, self-motivated, excellent communicator, seasoned, creative, loyal, dependable, on-time, reliable, quick study, a leader, pragmatic, organized, computer literate, self-starter, out-of-the box thinker, responsible for,* and similar words or phrases. These do not add value to the resume, and take up valuable space. Nor are they things recruiters search for in a resume. Let your accomplishments and power phrases speak to these traits. Although these may be traits that the hiring manager or company seeks of its candidates, they will not be believed on face value, but must be demonstrated in your resume statements of accomplishment and during an interview.

Finally, do not phrase your accomplishments in the first person: for example, *I develop, I wrote, I hired,* and so on. Also avoid using the passive voice when framing your statements: for example, *the process was completed* (the engineers completed the process), *50 people were hired in 30 days* (the department head hired 50 people in 30 days), *our team was approached by management* (management approached our team), and so on.

Summary or Profile

The summary or profile can be one of the most difficult parts of the resume to write. Most profiles add little value, and may limit the person's marketability to the broader market. If you are highly specialized in what you do, or what you want, this will work beautifully as a reverse filter.

If you can not add real value to your resume in the objective, consider skipping it altogether.

If you put a summary or profile statement at the beginning of your resume, it should be written after you have laid out your resume and developed your key words and power phrases. Keep in mind that this statement *is your chance to promote yourself* and should be an incentive for the reader to take a look at your whole resume. It is a written snapshot of who you are, your qualifications, and career interests. Take a look at everything you have written in your resume and see if you can create the real essence of you. Distill all your words and power phrases down to three or four sentences. Once again, avoid cliches, excessive adjectives, and often-used descriptors such as *seasoned professional, versatile manager, effective leader,* and so on.

Remember your networking "pitch" when writing the summary. Translate your verbal introduction into a written summary. It speaks to who you are and what you seek in your career. Most importantly it will be unique and unlike any of the other resumes the company or recruiter receives. Take a look at the following and see what a difference there is between summaries.

Everyone Else's:

"Seasoned compensation manager with 15 years experience designing and developing wage and salary plans, and incentives. Conduct surveys and recommend individual and position compensation changes. Skilled in application of advanced Excel spreadsheet tools and presentations, as well as database integration. Seek to apply my compensation know-how in a global consumer-products company where I can advance and grow."

Yours:

"Business-oriented human resources professional who is adept in leveraging employee results and retention through the design and application of innovative performance-based compensation and rewards programs. Possess strong market-assessment skills and ability to integrate computer technology and compensation data to create real-time management decision tools. Seek senior-level compensation-function leadership role requiring strong vision and strategy."

Everyone Else's:

"Veteran Materials Manager seeks Director of Purchasing position in the durable metals goods industry. Record of successfully negotiating vendor agreements, generating purchase orders, and containing parts price increases. Have hired and supervised buyers and clerks. Computer literate."

Yours:

"Supply Chain Manager with exceptional accomplishments in materials planning, procurement, logistics, inventory control, and product distribution. Highly respected for knowledge and experience in designing and rolling out *just-in-time* inventory and *e-procurement* systems. Continually applying new supply processes and computer software/systems to secure break-through results in production efficiencies and reduction in material costs."

Notice a difference between the two versions? One is often-used and uninspiring while the other is unique, refreshing, and packed with key words and power phrases. Which one do you think will better prompt one to read on? It is infrequent where someone reads the entire resume. Most resumes are a quick read and even then it may be just the summary statement. Executive recruiters often read the profile, glance at one's current job title and company (pedigree check!), and then go down or flip the page to see one's educational credentials (another pedigree check!). The latter also serves as a check on overall length of experience. Consequently, the summary or objective section may be the only shot you have at grabbing the reader's attention.

Chapter Worksheet

Although it is important to know what to cover in your letters and resumes, it is even more important to know how to express it. Key words and power phrases are critical. They turn your communications and career statements into impressive, articulate expressions of your skills, accomplishments, and know-how. These tools elevate you in the eyes of the reader and evoke positive decisions with respect to advancing you along the candidacy steps. You need to learn to "write what you mean" and "mean what you write." Work at becoming proficient in writing cover letters and composing your resume. Use the following questions to develop your writing strategies and you will get a *call to action* on behalf of the readers.

- ▶ The company (or recruitment firm) that you are contacting, what is it about?
- ▶ Specifically to whom are you writing? Do you know anything about the person?
- ▶ What is the objective of your letter?
- ▶ What do you want to say?
- ▶ How do you want to say it? What should you avoid (cliches, adjectives)?
- ▶ What words and power phrases are important in saying it?
- ▶ Is there a specific position? If so, how do you tie in and meet their needs?
- ▶ What is the industry? How well do you know it? Where can you get more information if you need to bone up?
- ▶ What is your expectation? Have you planned a call to action (for example, what do you want the reader to do?).
- ▶ What do you intend to do after sending the letter? How and when will you follow up?
- ▶ What key words and power phrases should you put in your resume?
- ▶ Are there stronger choices for the specific position?
- ▶ Can you articulate your accomplishments to include results?
- ▶ Can you provide metrics and other supporting data?
- ▶ What do you want your resume summary or profile to state?
- ▶ How can you state it so it is unique unto only you?

CHAPTER 3

Preparing for the Interview: Doing Your Homework

B eing prepared for an interview means knowing every thing about you and your work history. It means being comfortable explaining all that is on your resume and beyond. One best prepares for an interview by rehearsing the answers to every possible question that might be asked of you, and knowing how to inject the same information should the questions not be asked. This chapter will help you prepare phrases and answers to the questions you may experience in an interview.

Being prepared for an interview also means that you have thoroughly researched the company and the individuals you will be meeting, and that you have given thought to the questions you should be putting forward during the interview. The level, frequency, depth, and articulation with which you ask questions can be more revealing to the interviewer than your actual answers to his or her own questions. It relays what you know about the company and the job, as well as your desire to learn more. The converse is also applicable: to ask immaterial

questions, or to ask none at all, can be interpreted as not being prepared or not truly interested in the company and in the
job opportunity. So let's spend some time reviewing when and
how in the interview you should be asking questions, and how
you can prepare.

Researching Yourself

Yes, there is a process to follow when reviewing yourself,
your work history, work responsibilities, and accomplishments.
You become prepared by writing down (or word processing)
your entire history, chronologically, starting with your post-
high-school education and then moving to each employer. With
your schooling, put down what your major was and the courses
you took. Why? What did you learn? How have you applied
that knowledge in the workplace? What did you enjoy the
most? Least? For each of your employment periods list the
company, the job and title, the dates, and for whom you worked
(and title). What were your responsibilities? How did you learn
to do them? What was the most difficult part of the job? What
level of authority did you have? List all your achievements
and accomplishments. What were they? What was the end
result? How did you do it? How did you know? Who else was
involved? Why did you leave? Become fluent in talking about
each of the jobs and illustrating skills, competencies, or accomplishments that existed in every job.

Once you have culled all this information, reviewed it thoroughly, and rehearsed the answers to possible questions, you
are ready. The notes can be retrieved and revisited before
every new interview. It becomes, in a way, a primer on *you*
and your *work history*.

Researching the Company

The next thing you need to do prior to meeting with a
prospective employer is to learn everything you can about the

company, its products and/or services, the industry it is in, and its performance (financial and nonfinancial). The second thing you need to do is to learn as much as you can about the person with whom you will be interviewing, and to whom the position reports. Thirdly, you must research as much as you can about the position for which you are interviewing. Armed with insight about the company, the boss, and the job you can prepare intelligent questions which not only showplace *you*, but also help you gain important information to help you decide whether or not this company and job are right for you.

Let's cover company and industry information first. Today, you are very likely to find most or all of this online. One of the best places with which to start out is the company's Website. You can research the industry by going to an industry association Website, browsing competitors' sites, and turning to your local library's printed and electronic business directories. All this will take a bit of work, but it will pay off in droves. It should provide information on clients, customers, competitors, financials, trends, and so forth. If the company's stock is publicly traded, places such as *Yahoo! Finance* are great repositories of data about companies, key employees, the industry, and competitors. Documents filed by the company with the SEC (Securities Exchange Commission) are also available at *www.sec.gov/edgar.shtml*. EDGAR is an acronym for the Electronic Data Gathering, Analysis, and Retrieval system the SEC developed to store and retrieve important agency documents that companies are legally required to file on a periodic, scheduled, or incident-driven basis. This kind of research will help you identify strengths and weaknesses of the company, avoid some major pitfalls during the interview, and ask good questions that show understanding, insight, and interest. Company press releases are another excellent source of information, and a running history should be found on the Website. *Yahoo! Finance* also accumulates relevant press announcements.

In today's global world and international job market, your potential employer may be headquartered in another country on another continent. Webpages, articles, and documents may be in a foreign language and yet contain information vital to you. Make use of the many translation tools that reside on the Internet. Although the resulting transcript may not be perfect, it will give you the gist of what was written.

Researching the Individual

As is the case with scoping out the company, the Internet is an excellent first stop on your quest for information about the individual with whom you will be interviewing. Any of the major search engines (*Google*, *Yahoo*, *My Excite*, *Lycos*, *Altavista*, *MSN*, and so on) can, with proper search words, tell you if information exists or not. Experimenting with the individual's name and other identifying words such as city, state, company, organization, and so on, will help you narrow the number of listings you will need to peruse. Another search engine, *zoominfo.com*, is dedicated to tracking down information about people. It pulls up references to all who have that name and, with some additional effort, you can narrow down the number of hits. If you know the individual's email address, query it on one of the search engines. Articles by or about the individual, if they cite the person's e-mail for contact purposes, will surface. These can be symposium papers, press releases, conference reports, blogs, newspaper articles, association directories, and so on. All this information helps you know more about the person and provides talking points for when interviewing.

Don't overlook the company Website as a source of information about the person. Drop the name in the search box and see what is listed. The authors have come across numerous company Websites where new-hire notices, press releases, and so on, are posted. Some actually list staff directories exposing telephone numbers, e-mail addresses, and titles. Others have insightful information in the contact section. It is not uncommon for a company to put current and archived newsletters on its Website. They are full of articles about products, business initiatives, Qs and As, new-hire notices, and department features. All this is useful in learning more about the interviewer and the company.

Lastly, there is your existing network of contacts that may be able to tell you something about the individual, or know someone in the company who can. A review of your expansive contact list may reveal someone who can either help you first-hand, or by some manner of connectivity (that is, put out the request, "Who do you know at XYZ company?").

Researching the Job

Your third arena to research is the position for which you are applying. What is involved? What are the responsibilities? What are the recruiting specs (background expectations of the desired candidate)? Where does the position fit in the department and company hierarchy? What aspects of the job parallel those in your current position? What new duties or tasks are there? Is there something missing that normally is part of such a position? How complex is the job? What do you think you will need from the organization or the new boss in order to be effective in the job? The answers to these questions may reside right in the job description, or may need to be pursued during your interview.

In earlier times, it was often impossible to obtain a full job-description write-up. Today, however, it is not uncommon for it to be posted on the company's career page on its Website. E-mail makes it very convenient to request a copy from the recruiter, the hiring manager, or the HR department. Regardless of whether you have a copy of the position description or duties, tap your contacts (if you have any) at that company for additional insight into the department and the position.

All of the previously mentioned research is pertinent to improving your odds of success with your interview(s). Information and intelligent questioning are your allies in an interview. Today's job applicants are savvy and more informed than those of past years. In part, this is because of the myriad information available online today. Second, the number of individuals competing for the same position opening has grown exponentially because of how positions are advertised today. With job opportunities posted on company, recruiter, and state job-service Websites, professional association job boards, online conversions of newspaper classifieds, large job boards (such as *Monster* and *CareerBuilder.com*), plus professional networking groups that circulate jobs that were to have been "top secret," the word is definitely out and the savvy job hunter has found and applied to all that might be a fit. Electronic applications and responses are much easier than mailing a cover letter and resume. The bottom line is that more people are applying for more jobs. No longer are you competing with 15 or 20 other qualified applicants, but possibly hundreds or even thousands. You have to be prepared, or you will lose out despite having the qualifications and interest.

Before going into an interview, you need to be aware of a few things. Many people who conduct interviews have limited experience, or have their own personal style of interviewing. They have not been taught how to ask probing questions in order to extract the information they need. Instead, they engage in conversations, ask questions with obvious answers, give statements and expect responses, or wait for you to lead the interview. All of these situations offer you the advantage. If you lead the interview, ask great questions, and converse well, you are a step ahead of the other candidates. Other interviewers know what to ask, but sometimes rely on simple questions to see how you respond. Either way, you must take advantage of these unstructured approaches by putting detail and structure in your answers. You must be in the driver's seat.

For every unprepared, poorly trained interviewer out there, there are also some great interviewers who have honed their interviewing skills. They are adept at asking open-ended questions (questions that require more than a "yes" or "no" answer) and they may be experts in asking situation/outcome questions. These are questions that ask you about a situation relating to a specific topic, skill, action, and so on, and what you did, how you did it (perhaps even why you did it), and what the end result was. You will need to be prepared.

Opening Phrases

These are the phrases that are used in the very beginning of the interview process. After going through the standard greetings, "Good morning, how are you? How was your drive? Would you like some coffee?" and so forth, it's time to jump right in. Right at this point is one of your best opportunities, while the meeting is still conversational, to gain valuable information and provide information that you want to include.

Your questions or statements will show understanding and insight. You will appear to be well-prepared for your interview, well-informed, inquisitive, intelligent, and interested in the position. This can make all the difference.

Bad Questions or Conversational Statements:

▶ "What does your company do?"
▶ "How many people are in the company?"
▶ "I just want to tell you at the onset that this job is meant for me. It has my name on it."
▶ "Who are your competitors?"
▶ "How long does it take you to deliver your product?"
▶ "What are you benefits like?"
▶ "It has been quite a while since I have done an interview so please excuse me if I am nervous."

▸ "I am not certain if I am right for this job, but I figured I would still go through the interviewing."

Good Questions or Conversational Statements:

▸ "What are some of the biggest difficulties you have in developing new products?"

▸ "What differentiates you from your competitors?"

▸ "I am delighted to be here, as I see a strong fit between my background and your job needs."

▸ "How do the features and benefits of your products compare to others in the marketplace?"

▸ "How did this position opening come about?"

▸ "While having a cup of coffee in the cafeteria I noticed everyone seemed to be upbeat. Why is that?"

▸ "I am looking forward to this discussion as our companies have a lot in common."

▸ "How is your job search going so far? Where are you in the process? "

▸ "Tell me about yourself, when you joined the company, and what you enjoy about your job."

All questions and statements should help you steer the conversation to areas in which you wish to immediately make a positive impression or to convey important information about you and the job that may not otherwise come up in the interview. However, some interviewers may jump right in to the formal part of the interview thus closing off any initial opportunities to ask questions or make a statement. If that occurs, don't try to force the interview in a different direction. You should have ample time later to ask questions and engage in a closing conversation.

A Tip When Asking Questions

When you ask a question in an interview...wait for the answer! Do not offer help, clarify, give suggestions, or add any more information. Just ask a question and wait. This will provide the information you need. Clarifying and giving help of any kind not only sabotages your question, but it makes you look ineffective. People often make this mistake out of nervousness, or to fill in an awkward silence. Don't fall into that trap. Similarly, when a broad or unclear question is asked of you, don't be silent or jump into an answer that may not be germane. Instead, respond with a clarifying question such as, "Are you asking me to name the key attributes of developing traceable computer code?", or "If I understand your question correctly, you want me to tell you how I prepare for a committee presentation, is that correct?" Never repeat, verbatim, the interviewer's question but, instead, reframe it or paraphrase the question. You may be able to steer the answer to a slightly different topic than the interviewer intended just by restating the question to your favor, or by shifting a broad question to a specific answer: "When I think of the many decisions I have had to make, I most remember those that were required under stressful situations. For example...."

Phrases for Resume Questions

Resume questions are questions that are generated using your resume as a springboard. They are used to probe deeper into your experience, skills, and attributes you have listed on your resume. For this reason, no resume question should ever come as a surprise. Every bullet on your resume begs a resume question with a simple addition of what, when, where, how, with whom, or why and what was the end result (metric). Here are some examples:

Resume Bullet: Increased revenue by 120 percent in region in first year.

Questions: "What did you do specifically that increased revenue by 120 percent? How does that compare to the others in your department?"

Resume Bullet: Leveraged brand image through television and online campaigns.

Questions: "What were the results of your campaigns? How did those results compare to similar campaigns the company ran?"

Resume Bullet: Created new technique to increase efficiency of water flow.

Questions: "How did you come up with that solution? What were the alternatives you considered?"

Resume Bullet: Grew the generic brand sales at a 20 percent compounded rate.

Questions: "What was the overall market-growth rate compared to yours? What single thing made the greatest difference in achieving this rate of growth?"

As you can see from the previous examples, the interviewer seeks to gain a deeper understanding of your skills and accomplishments. If you fail to anticipate these questions, you will be less likely to give an answer that presents you in the best possible light. Fortunately anticipating resume questions is not that difficult.

Go over every bullet in your resume and identify every possible question that could be asked. Become comfortable reciting the what, when, where, how, why, and who or "with whom." If your resume does not state the metrics (time, dollars, percentages, or other tangible results) be prepared to cite such in an interview. Do your homework!

Resume-Question Warning

Many interviewees begin their answers to questions related to their responsibilities with, "I had to...." This conveys a poor impression to the interviewer. It gives the impression that one didn't like doing those duties. It also shows a lack of ownership and pride in the work that was done. Always start you answers with "I was responsible for...", or "I had responsibility for...", or "I managed...", or even, "I was in charge of...."

Where appropriate and real, add adjectives such as *total*, *complete, entire*, and so on. "I had sole responsibility for compiling and reporting the quality statistics," or "I was the senior manager entrusted with making on-site construction materials changes."

Phrases for Job-Description/ Duties Statements

Job duties questions are asked to see if there is a match with your background and the statement of responsibilities, duties, or tasks performed in the job description (and job!). Job descriptions (remember you researched what is on the job description for the position for which you are applying) contain a listing of key duties, such as, "Schedules subassembly production in accordance with master sales schedule and material availability." The interviewer may explore your ability to perform this duty by asking you directly or indirectly about your experiences in this area. For example, "Share with me how you generate a master-production schedule for your generator line," "Tell me about a time when you were having difficulty with production-schedule interruptions. What was the problem? How did you correct it?", "What is the most difficult element when it comes to balancing your production schedule?", or "Overall, what is your production line downtime rate? What are the top factors influencing up time?"

In preparation for your interview take the job description for this position or, if not available, then utilize the recruitment advertisement which lists the key responsibilities and correlate each responsibility statement to what you currently do in your present job or past job. Make notes of what you have done. The what's, how's, why's, time frames, end results, and so on. This is very similar to the exercises you did with your "resume bullets" earlier in this book.

Phrases for Experience Questions

Experience questions are asked of you to learn more about your skills and to assess your competencies. Every job description cites the experiences required to be a candidate, and a good interviewer will want to verify your own experiences to see if there is a match. Experience questions come mainly from two sources. First, your experience may be determined through resume questions, as previously described. Job descriptions are the other main source. Assuming you are already prepared to answer just about any kind of resume question thrown at you, you are partly prepared for experience questions. All that remains is to study the job description to see what experience questions the manager may ask based on the job experience requirements.

Job-Description Bullet: Job requires proficiency in sterile product sampling.

Question: "What kind of experience do you have with sterile-product sampling?"

Answer: "More than 50 percent of the projects I am currently working on involve sterile product sampling, for which I am responsible."

Experience-Question Warning

Some managers have very short job descriptions, or none at all. In this case, these questions can be generated based on the manager's perception of the position's needs. This will make it harder to anticipate what questions the manager might ask. Your best shortcut to identifying what experience questions may be asked is to revisit the recruitment or help-wanted ad, which usually contains a few experience statements. Another approach is to ask the recruiter, if one is involved, for the experience specs. Regardless, why not ask the interviewer what he or she wants to see in the candidates in terms of experience?

To better aid you in responding to resume, job description, and experience questions Chapter 5 contains tips and phrases for specific functional areas.

Phrases for Self-Appraisal Questions

These can be some of the trickiest questions to deal with. Often interviewers ask these types of questions in order to eliminate the candidates with the least experience. Although it may be tempting to tell the interviewer that your skills are better than they are in order to avoid being cut from the candidate pool, it would be unwise. Ultimately, the employer is going to find out exactly what your skills are, and a nasty surprise for them won't be good for you either. We suggest that candidates give an honest answer with a positive spin. Tell the employer that you are very interested in this area, what your current skills are, and how you intend to improve them.

The other type of self-appraisal question is even trickier. These questions are asked in a way that the employer intends for your answer to evaluate your weaknesses. Here are two examples. "What area do you need the most improvement in?", or "What do you think is your greatest drawback as a candidate for this position?" Whatever you do, do not deprecate yourself or diminish your skills in any way. First, tell your interviewer(s) something positive about you, then either tell them what they already know, or give them something that is completely unrelated to the job at hand.

For example, if you are entry level, a good answer might be, "I am very interested in this job, but as you can see from my resume, I don't yet have a lot of experience." As you can see, you gave them nothing. The answer didn't say anything negative about your skills, attributes, motivation level, or anything else. It did, however, satisfy his or her question because you gave an honest answer. You did tell them that you are interested in the job, but little more that they don't already know. The answer you gave them gives them no additional insight into the negatives of having you as an employee. You told them what they already knew before they even agreed to interview you. That you are an entry-level candidate, looking for an entry-level job, with entry-level experience.

Another example (this one appropriate for a mid-career candidate seeking an electrical engineering job) might be, "You know, while I am very experienced in my area of engineering, I really haven't had a lot of experience in the other areas." Once again, this gives them nothing. They aren't seeking to hire this candidate to do civil or mechanical engineering, but as an electrical engineer. Whether or not he has experience in unrelated areas to his job is totally irrelevant, but this answer does satisfy the question.

Phrases for Situational Questions

Situational questions are "what if" questions. These are phrased as either "What would you do if...?" or "What have you done in...situation?" The purpose of this type of question is to determine your ability to handle specific, relevant situations. They are also used to find out the quality of your general decision-making skills. The best way to anticipate situational questions that may come up is to review all the situations that may occur on a day-to-day basis with this position. Although you may not be able to anticipate every question that may come up, you may find that many of the answers you do come up with might be applicable to some degree.

Good answers for situational questions will vary greatly depending on your industry, your role within the firm, and even the company's own philosophy. For example, the decision an aircraft pilot should make in the event of encountering wind shear on short, final approach is totally unrelated to the decision a flight attendant should make in the same situation.

Additionally, the decision the pilot makes may be drastically different depending on his or her function. A military pilot on a special assignment of critical importance, who needs to land immediately in order for the mission to be successful, might make a different decision than a commercial airline pilot (who is not under such pressure) faced with the same problem.

Based on the variable nature of answers for this type of question, there are a few approaches you can take. When confronted with this type of question, answer as honestly as you can. If his or her philosophies are irreconcilably different from yours, this is not the place for you to work. A good answer can show how you have handled situations in the past, and/or your previous employers' policy regarding that type of situation, or other supporting facts as to why you did what you did. To soften the impact of the answer that may be different from what the hiring manager was looking for, a great follow-up question is, "What is the procedure for handling this type of situation here?" This shows that you are not stuck in your ways, and that you want to learn his or her philosophies in order to do business in the way he or she prescribes.

Phrases for Stress Questions

Stress questions come in many flavors. Some are not questions at all, but statements. Others are neither questions nor statements, but situations the prospective employer might put you in. They can be just about anything that will surprise you, attempt to evoke an emotional response, or throw you off-kilter. The purpose of a stress question is to see how you work under pressure, or how you deal with a difficult situation. I break them down into the three major categories previously mentioned. Here are some examples:

Questions:
▶ "Why should we hire you?"
▶ "I see you have been with your current company for quite some without moving up. Why is that?"

▶ "We have quite a number of excellent candidates for this job. Why do you feel that you are qualified?"

▶ "What kind of problems do you have with your current boss?"

▶ "Do you consider yourself to be a lucky person?"

Situations:

▶ Being kept waiting for an inappropriately long time.

▶ Being seated opposite a large number of interviewers.

▶ A long period of uncomfortable silence.

▶ A strange noise (for example, computers/technology/phone beeps, alerts, or other sounds).

Statements:

▶ "I am not convinced that you can deal with difficult customers."

▶ "I don't think you really want this job."

▶ "There are things you will need to change in order to work here."

▶ "Your experience does not seem to be directly related to the requirements of this position."

Whatever the form of stress question, don't stress out! The best way to answer or respond is to keep calm and figure out what the interviewer(s) is hoping to find out about you. From there you can formulate your response. From these examples, a long period of silence should remain unbroken for a very long time. Only after several minutes, you might say, "Shall we continue?" This shows that you can handle such situations without falling to pieces, and that you will take control and get things back on track when necessary.

I find that stress questions usually tell very little about the candidate that is relevant for my purposes. I have developed other methods that I have found to help me gain better information. Although I am not an advocate of stress questions and I don't use them when I interview candidates, there are still some employers who do feel that they are valuable. For this reason, be prepared.

Phrases for Insulting Questions

Insulting questions are rare indeed. Although I believe them to be totally ineffective in most situations, there are still some employers who feel that they are important. And though I understand that some jobs do require employees to deal with irate customers, and even insulting behavior and comments, I think there are better ways to see the interviewee's reaction than in the interview. Despite that, and because some employers still use this method, let's prepare.

Insults:

▶ "I find your manner of dress to be inappropriate for an interview. Women should wear suits with a skirt."

▶ "I don't think you are hardworking enough for me to consider you."

▶ "You can't even.... Why should I hire you?"

▶ "Why would I even consider you for this position?"

When confronted with an insult, such as those previously mentioned, there are several immediate options. Getting angry isn't one of them. This puts the employer in total control of you, and that is unacceptable. You can choose to either move forward with the interview assuming it's a test, or decide that this is unacceptable and firmly, yet politely, end the interview immediately. The latter shows dignity and integrity, but the former can also be achieved with dignity and integrity.

Before answering the insult or question, here are a few phrases to precede your answer with:

Responses:

▸ "I find that to be highly offensive, but I would like to respond anyway."

▸ "I respect your feelings, but I completely disagree. Let me explain why...."

▸ "I am very surprised; how did you draw that conclusion?"

Insulting-Question Tip

Remember, whether you get this job or not, you are a professional. Always act as the professional you are. Do not lose your composure, especially in the face of adversity. When someone other that you acts in an inappropriate or unprofessional manner, that does not mean that you should, too. Distance yourself from it and show the stark contrast between the two types of behavior. You will benefit by doing this throughout your career.

Phrases for Puzzle Questions

Some interviewers use a puzzle when evaluating a candidate. They are often in the form of riddles or logic problems. Some of these problems will have a solvable correct answer, whereas others have no real answer. In either case the approach is the same. After confirming that it is not just a rhetorical question, such as, "Do you know how many turkeys we gave away last year for Thanksgiving?" take on the question and do not give up easily. If you are asked if you want to give up, ask for another try. Keep working through it, draw diagrams, and do whatever is necessary to come up with the best answer you can.

The purpose of this type of question is less about getting the answer right than showing your ability to analyze the situation, work through the problem, and offer a solution. People who just give up usually are eliminated as viable candidates for the job. Here are some examples of puzzle questions.

Puzzle question: "How many gas stations are there in the United States?"

Process and answer: "Let's see...there are two gas stations in my town, and the population is.... Assuming this ratio of people to gas stations remains constant throughout the United States, there must be approximately...gas stations in the country."

Other Sample Puzzle Questions:

▸ "How many cars are in the United States?"

▸ "With an unlimited supply of water, how would you precisely measure out 3 quarts of water using a 4-quart bucket and a 9-quart bucket?

▸ "Which way should a key turn to open a lock?"

Phrases for Compensation Questions

Questions about compensation can be very dangerous. Hiring managers often ask what salary you are hoping to achieve. If you ask for too much, you will probably be removed from consideration for the position. However, if you ask for too little, you might get it. If you are working with a recruiter, you can refer the interviewer to the recruiter, because he or she will not have the same problems you do. The recruiter is an expert and should know what you are worth, what you want, and what the company will to pay. If he or she goes too high, they can come back with a lower number and no harm is done.

If, however, you are representing yourself, there are a few approaches you can take. You can mention that you want fair pay, but emphasize that what you really want is the right job with the right company. Also emphasize that you are confident that should the hiring manager make an offer, you know he or she will make an offer that makes sense. Another answer is, "I am hoping for your best offer." Additionally, if you do have a firm number in mind that you really do need to achieve is, you might say, "It's going to take [salary expectation] to get me through the door."

Questions about salary history are more difficult to evade. You can point out several facts if the salary for the position is lower than the one you came from. Here are a few examples:

Example #1:

"My salary was.... However, keep in mind that my base was only...."

Example #2:

"At [your company name], I was paid.... But compensation is only part of the whole picture. Stability, prestige, work environment, and quality of life are very important to me. Those factors outweigh the importance of a higher salary."

Short Phrases

For following up after a question, some short phrases can be very helpful. Keep in mind that questions drive and control the conversation, whereas statements add information. Both are important (in the proper amount) in order to share the information you want and gain the information you need, as well as allow you to maintain some level of control.

People who are in an interview often forget that interviewing is a two-sided interaction. They get so focused on "interviewing well" and trying to impress the interviewer that they forget that they also need to be satisfied with the job, responsibilities, work environment, peers, and employer in order to accept the job if it is offered. It is critical that you make sure that you want the job if it is offered. This information should be gained from the interview. Following are sample short phrases you can use after answering a question to either regain control and deepen your understanding of the firm, or to show that you have the ability to do the job you are discussing.

Short-Question Phrases

▶ "Why is that?"

▶ "How do you view that?"

▶ "How should that be achieved?"

▶ "What kind of results has that provided?"

Short-Statement Phrases

▶ "I can certainly handle that."

▶ "I particularly enjoy that aspect."

▶ "I have a lot of experience in that area."

▶ "That is similar to what I do currently."

Tip: Short-statement phrases should often, but not always, be followed up with a question.

Closing Phrases

All good things must come to an end. This includes interviews. After information has been exchanged and questions have been answered, it's time to end the interview. Here are some phrases to ask at the end of the interview that will either give you more insight into the company and its hiring decision, and/or help to drive home the point that you are right for the job.

Closing Phrases

▶ "Based on what you now know about me and what we have discussed, how do you feel I would do in this position?"

▶ "What are your thoughts about my fit with your organization?"

▶ "Are there any concerns you have about me in regards to this position?"

▸ "I really like what I have seen today and I am very interested in the position. What is the next step?"

▸ "Shall I call you toward the end of week to follow up?"

Chapter Worksheet

▸ List the resume questions you anticipate.

▸ Based on the job description, what are some experience questions the interviewer might ask?

▸ How would you answer some common self-appraisal questions?

▸ What are some answers to situational questions you might face?

▸ How would you deal with an insult?

▸ What is your plan if compensation questions come up?

▸ How would you go about answering a puzzle or riddle?

▸ What opening phrases might you use?

▸ What closing questions might be appropriate?

CHAPTER 4

Job-Specific Phrases

This chapter has specific areas that you will want to accentuate for the job area you are seeking employment. Although these phrases are generally the areas you will want to talk about the most, each company has its own criteria it uses to evaluate candidates. Look through other sections to see if there are additional areas you may want to discuss, depending on either the specific job, or company you are interviewing with.

Warning: Whenever you offer a phrase that is intended to show that you have a certain attribute, be prepared with examples. Many interviewers are firm believers that if you cannot offer recent examples off the top of your head, that you probably have not displayed that attribute recently.

Sales Phrases

If you are a sales professional, whether its inside sales (inbound or outbound), outside sales, or field sales, employers want to see many of the same things. Similarly, if a large portion of your job includes some level of selling or convincing, this section is also for you. Finally, some companies have a culture of sales, in which they feel that selling is part of every job. Once again, this section should help.

Although sales managers may look for different things, such as personality, selling style, past experience, and so forth, there are also many constants. These constants outweigh the importance of the other attributes a particular employer may be looking for. Here are a few:

Internal Motivation

Employers look for sales professionals they perceive as being generally motivated individuals. People with this attribute tend to be easy to motivate externally (with rewards, contests, commissions, and so on) as it is consistent with their internal workings. Although it is very difficult to demonstrate how motivated you are, showing examples of your tenacity gives very compelling evidence of your level of motivation. If you are a person who plays to win, tell the interviewer exactly that.

Internal-motivation phrase: "If you give me the chance, you will very quickly see how motivated I am."

Internal-motivation phrase: "I know you will see that my level of internal motivation is very high."

Internal-motivation phrase: "The thrill of closing a sale is so powerful, I'll do whatever is necessary to get there."

Internal-motivation phrase: "In 'sales ability' tests, I always score very high in motivation."

Attitude

A positive attitude goes a very long way in sales. With many "maybes," "call me laters," and hard prospects, employers may feel that someone lacking a positive attitude is going to have a much harder time succeeding. There are so many ways to show the positive attitude you want them to see. Smiling goes a long way. Not only does it show your positive attitude, it will make you feel more positive, and this will shine through. Make sure you phrase most things you say in positive way. Talk about the benefits of jobs you have had, and the things you learned and enjoyed. Even if you are cornered into speaking about something that was negative, mention the positive things that came from it.

Attitude phrase: "I have learned some important lessons in every phase of my career."

Attitude phrase: "I really enjoy sales and the challenges it offers."

Attitude phrase: "It has been so exciting to meet you and see everything that your company can do. Given the chance, I know I will prosper here."

Attitude phrase: "My positive attitude spills over to others on the sales team."

Sales Ability

Your sales technique and style are definitely going to be topics of conversation. Every sales professional has his or her own style. As long as it works for you, go with it. Sales education, however, is something you gain. Make sure to mention sales seminars and in-house training as well as books you have read. Talk about how you have used these tools and how they benefited you. When asked about technique, tell the interviewer what you have used in the past and why it was effective, but make sure to let them know that you want to continue to grow, and ask how things are done at their firm (as you are flexible). As long as you have the core skills, getting up to speed with their methodologies won't take long at all.

Sales-ability phrase: "What sales techniques work well for your company?"

Sales-ability phrase: "What do you expect of your sales personnel?"

Sales-ability phrase: "I am very familiar with several sales styles. What kind of style works best in your industry?"

Tenacity

There are few attributes that are as important as tenacity. Employers love salespeople who don't give up. You can show that you are tenacious by telling an anecdote about closing a particularly difficult sale despite all kinds of adversity. As mentioned previously, make sure you keep the positive tone and talk about the feelings of accomplishment you experienced with this challenge.

Tenacity phrase: "Sometimes the hardest challenges drive me the most."

Tenacity phrase: "I just don't believe in giving up."

Tenacity phrase: "Each no just brings me closer to a yes."

Tenacity phrase: "I always look for ways to satisfy the customer."

Energy Level

Energy creates energy, just as negative energy creates more negative energy. Employers fear with each hire that a new employee with a poor energy level can damage the entire office's ethos. Conversely, an energetic employee will add more energy to the office. For this reason, have several cups of coffee, if needed, before the interview, but go in with energy and excitement.

Energy-level phrase: "I am very excited to start on the projects we discussed."

Energy-level phrase: "You will find from my references that my output was the highest in the department."

Energy-level phrase: "I like to leave at the end of the day with a feeling of achievement and accomplishment."

Energy-level phrase: "Little slows me down."

Ability to Create Excitement

Great sales professionals can create excitement and add value to even mundane products. With an already-great product, these same people can add even more excitement. Try practicing by thinking about how you might try to sell something unexciting such as a pencil, pen, or coffee maker.

Ability-to-create-excitement phrase: "If I believe in and am excited about a product, I will excite others."

Ability-to-create-excitement phrase: "More than features and benefits, clients' emotions play a big part in a successful sale."

Ability-to-create-excitement phrase: "People always see me as the cheerleader, as I am continually excited with the prospects for new business."

Passion

Passion makes all the difference in sales. When people are passionate, they tend to have a better attitude, are more tenacious, and have a higher energy level. Show the employer your passion for the industry, product, or company through your attitude and energy level. You can even tell them how passionate you are.

Passion phrase: "I love the thrill of selling."

Passion phrase: "If it's a great product, I can sell it!"

Passion phrase: "There are few fields that are as exciting as...."

Passion phrase: "I have an unquenchable passion for...."

Ability to Close

Sales managers need people who can follow up, follow up some more, and even more...and close the sale. Without this ability, all the passion, sales ability, and other attributes won't result in a sale. You can show good ability in this area by talking about your past results. Tell about the increase you caused in sales in your territory, awards you won, your ranking in your department, or other increases you have caused. Cite examples of your most difficult sale(s), and what you had to do in order to close.

Ability-to-close phrase: "Without a proper close, there is no sale."

Ability-to-close phrase: "It's very easy to evaluate my closing ability. Just look at my numbers!"

Ability-to-close phrase: "I have one of the highest conversion rates in my group."

Tip: Getting a third-party endorsement (such as a reference from a former employer) can be a powerful tool to show off your positive attributes.

Marketing Phrases

More areas of business are being labeled *marketing*. Included under the marketing umbrella are: branding, promotional marketing, market research, advertising, direct mail, events and meetings, media, marketing communications, corporate standards, public relations, and so on. Some people even call sales positions marketing. For our purposes, we are only dealing with the areas of marketing that are fairly universal.

You need to show that you can add more value than the next person. Budgets are finite, and top management looks to marketing to achieve the very best return on each of its marketing efforts. The following are some areas that will probably come up:

Analysis

Analyzing data is critical in order to make the right choices. The numbers can lie, so it's also important to see what's behind the numbers.

Analysis phrase: "I try to look at not only the numbers, but what's behind them in order to make the best decision."

Analysis phrase: "Sometimes something looks great until you really take a long, hard look at the numbers."

Analysis phrase: "The biggest issue I look at is what the numbers are really measuring, and how that's relevant to us."

Analysis phrase: "Focus groups have proven to be strong indicators of our product's market success."

Creativity

Thinking outside of the box can create some of the best results. What you know and what you can find out and think up are a big part of the equation.

Creativity phrase: "It's coming up with that unique solution that excites me."

Creativity phrase: "I really enjoy looking at things in a different way than others."

Creativity phrase: "My friends say that I have a unique approach to just about everything."

Brand

Understanding the brand, where it is, and where it needs to go makes all the difference. Careful brand stewardship is key for any established brand, whereas leveraging is more important for a growing brand.

Brand phrase: "I have a lot of experience with brands. I can be sensitive to the brand while achieving your needs."

Brand phrase: "I understand the importance of proper brand stewardship."

Brand phrase: "I was instrumental in creating the new branding campaign."

Brand phrase: "The brand studies I have launched in the past have shown that...."

Decision-Making

Once you have all the information you need, showing that you can decide which message, vehicle, or mode you want to go with, and backing it up with that data shows good decision-making. This can best be shown through anecdotes about past decisions you made, and why you made them. Just make sure that the anecdotes you share resulted in superior performance or results.

Accounting/Financial Phrases

People entrusted with this kind of responsibility can be one of the company's greatest assets, but they can also bring irreparable harm the firm. For this reason, trust is one of the biggest factors that goes into hiring someone in this field.

Integrity

With access to certain information, it is often tempting for less-ethical people to use this knowledge for their own gain. This can have disastrous results for both the individual and the company. Also there may be times when one is asked to alter the numbers. Showing your integrity is a must.

Integrity phrase: "The soonest I can start is.... I feel that I have an obligation to my current employer and I want to treat them in a very fair and honorable manner."

Integrity phrase: "Before I start with you, I want to make certain that I have fulfilled all of my commitments to my former boss."

Integrity phrase: "I have a reputation for being honest and honorable, and always taking the moral high ground."

Communication

Whatever the state of the company, top management needs accurate information in as close to a real-time basis as possible so they can make the best decisions based on the facts. Regardless of how this information is transmitted, good written and oral communication can make all the difference to a hiring manager.

Communication phrase: "I try to get the information you need in as close to real time as possible."

Communication phrase: "I know you rely on the right information to make decisions. I can make sure that the information is precise."

Communication phrase: "I take pride in my oral and written communication skills."

Communication phrase: "I am extremely comfortable in front of audiences and executive boards."

Good With Numbers

This goes without saying, because numbers are the main tool you work with.

Good-with-numbers phrase: "I find working with numbers to be quite natural for me."

Good-with-numbers phrase: "I have always closed the monthly books on time."

Good-with-numbers phrase: "I enjoy the analysis part of the monthly results and variances."

Budgeting

Planning, projecting, and identifying expenses, and monitoring their progress are very important elements of the job.

Budgeting phrase: "I try to list every expense imaginable in an accurate way."

Budgeting phrase: "When the project starts, you can be assured that I will stay on top of it to make sure we track all expenses and stay on target."

Budgeting phrase: "I am experienced enough to ensure realistic and accurate budgeting."

Forecasting

Executives depend on accurate forecasting when they make decisions. These same executives count on you to have the skills to forecast correctly.

Forecasting phrase: "I have always been able to forecast results within a few percentage points of the actual results."

Forecasting phrase: "When I make projections, I can show the outcome of several different scenarios."

Forecasting phrase: "My rough estimates of projects have always been within 5 percent of the actual results."

Willingness to Roll up Your Sleeves and Pitch In

Because accounting and financial positions are so critical, sometimes, for unforeseen reasons, unexpected needs will come up. This can happen because someone left the department, is out on vacation, was promoted, or fell ill. Alternatively, it may be due to a financial crisis. For this reason, managers need people to be flexible, work the extra hours to fill in for someone, or finish a monthly closing. You have to do whatever is necessary as a part of the job.

Willingness-to-roll-up-your-sleeves-and-pitch-in phrase: "It's not about me or you; it's about the requirements of the company and getting the job done."

Willingness-to-roll-up-your-sleeves-and-pitch-in phrase: "I know the importance of doing the monthly closing on time, and that it always calls for extra effort and time."

Human Resources Phrases

Human resources has many roles in a company. Because human capital is usually either the number-one or number-two line item on the balance sheet, it's management is critical to a company's success.

Conflict Resolution

When internal issues arise, human resources is expected to step in and help resolve them. It's important that you show that you can see both sides of the story, document the facts, and work towards a solution.

Conflict-resolution phrase: "I enjoy working through issues and helping to find a middle ground."

Conflict-resolution phrase: "I try to see both sides of the disagreement in order to understand what potential solutions might work."

Conflict-resolution phrase: "It is very rewarding to gain a high level of consensus among dueling parties."

Recruitment

Companies are made up of people. For better or worse, the firm is only as good as the people who work there. One of the biggest areas you can add value is to recruit better, smarter, faster, and cheaper than the next person.

Recruitment phrase: "I work very hard to get the very best people for the job."

Recruitment phrase: "I work collaboratively with the hiring manager to ensure that we get the right employee to fill each position."

Recruitment phrase: "You will see that I can keep the cost per hire down to a minimum."

Recruitment phrase: "I look to uncover, approach, and hire industry leaders in my recruitment campaigns."

Compensation

Compensation is key to recruitment, employee satisfaction, and productivity. Show your understanding of both the

salary portion of compensation as well as the other components (vacation, health benefits, and other programs).

Compensation phrase: "Executive compensation is a specialty of mine."

Compensation phrase: "I'm a believer in 'fair pay' and I
have helped achieve it in the past."

Compensation phrase: "Having human capital does have
its risks. It is a necessary liability. Showing that you know the
rules can help your potential employer understand that you
can help to mitigate these risks."

Compensation phrase: "Regulations are getting stricter every year. I can help you avoid costly errors."

Compensation phrase: "I have remained on the cutting
edge when it comes to compliance despite all the changes."

Annual-Review Process

In order for employees to improve, they need accurate,
fair, reliable, and unbiased appraisals. The managers who perform these appraisals will need assistance and supervision to
make certain that the process is performed according to company guidelines.

Annual-review-process phrase: "I understand the tension
an annual review can cause, and I try to minimize it to get
great results."

Annual-review-process phrase: "I have used many systems
in the past and understand many of the pluses and minuses of
each."

Annual-review-process phrase: "Difficult appraisals really
don't faze me."

Documentation

All issues must be documented. It helps create a fair system in which there is backup data to support matters at hand.
It also helps to prevent a feeling of biased treatment and can

reduce the firm's risk of costly lawsuits. Although the process is different from company to company, you may need to demonstrate that you understand the fundamentals.

Labor or Employee Relations

Because employees are such an essential part of almost any business, how they are dealt with is critical. This can be especially true when unions are involved.

Labor/employee-relations phrase: "I have an open-door policy and I encourage people to slip in and discuss issues that affect them."

Labor/employee-relations phrase: "Listening carefully to an employee's concerns is often almost as important as finding the right solutions for them."

Labor/employee-relations phrase: "I always try to act promptly on issues employees bring to my attention."

Labor/employee-relations phrase: "I strive to deal with everyone in a fair and equal manner."

Creative Arts Phrases

Branding, marketing, publicity, and advertising can drive a product. For it to work, the strategy has to make sense. Every detail, from the big picture to each little piece has to come together properly to form the larger marketing campaign.

Innovation

Each design project is different. The goals, products, audience, forum, technology, fashions, and conventions all change. For this reason, creative types need to constantly innovate. Yesterday's design may no longer be valid for today's audience. When you meet with a hiring manager, your portfolio will tell a lot about how innovative you are, but additionally, here are some phrases that might help:

Innovation phrase: "I try to push the envelope to the edge of what's possible to create with today's technology."

Innovation phrase: "When no solution is available with current technology, it just means that we need to develop new techniques."

Innovation phrase: "The most exciting thing about design is how wide open it is. Each project can have thousands of possible solutions and it's the creation of that totally new solution that's a thrill for me."

Computer Skills

Years ago, word processing, calculations, and creative arts were totally different. There were no computers involved in the process. Everything was done mechanically or on paper. However, today, almost all creative work, number "crunching," and word processing is done on the computer. The right computer skills are an absolute prerequisite to getting a job in the creative field. Candidates need to be truly proficient in all the related and necessary software packages in their field. Because hiring managers are usually savvy computer users, too, there is no longer much chance to fake it. These skills must shine through in your portfolio and speak for themselves.

Computer-skills phrase: "I work with...version of...software."

Computer-skills phrase: "I am very familiar with the changes in the new version of...."

Computer-skills phrase: "I am proficient in...."

Computer-skills phrase: "I am regarded as an advanced Access user."

Reliability and Timeliness

Although there are many great creative professionals in the world, only the best are able to produce great results in the time frame discussed. When deadlines aren't practical these same top people are able to express what is feasible in a given period of time. This enables the manager to make better decisions. He or she can add freelancers or other resources, cut back the scale of the project, or extend the deadline when possible. Most importantly, it allows the manager to communicate accurately with clients, vendors, or other interested parties, and prevents damage to the manager's reputation for achieving effective results.

Customer-Service Phrases

Customer service is where customers go when they have a problem. They are often frustrated, or have questions or concerns. A good customer-service representative can assist the customer and help bolster the company's reputation. Because no product can be 100-percent trouble-free, the biggest difference between the good and the not-so-good companies is how they handle problems that arise. Because customer-service representatives are just that, representatives, they *are* the company as far as the customer is concerned. Few positions offer the potential to show the customer what the company is all about as well as customer service does. If you can show the manager that you will make the company look great, the job should be yours.

Customer Focus

This component is what customer service is all about. It's about focusing on the customers' needs and making sure that they are given the solutions and tools they need for the product to work for them.

Customer-focus phrase: "I enjoy working with the customer to help them see how great the company and products are."

Customer-focus phrase: "For me, it's all about the customer. They are the lifeblood of the company and I want them to be satisfied."

Conflict Management

The essence of customer service is managing customer problems and issues. From these problems, conflicts may arise. Show the potential employer that you can defuse these issues and get the customer to become well-satisfied.

Conflict-management phrase: "I work towards solutions to customer issues that work for both the customer and the firm."

Conflict-management phrase: "Irate customers present a special challenge, and I have a calming effect with them."

Follow-Through

Show that you will follow up with the client on problems that are being dealt with, to ensure his or her satisfaction.

Follow-through phrase: "For me, the job isn't finished until the customer is satisfied and signs off."

Follow-through phrase: "When I tell a customer that I am going to do something, I make sure it is done, and done right."

Creating Solutions

Although there are many set procedures you can use to assist customers with their problems, new issues turn up almost daily. Even though your manager should be able to help in this area, sometimes, it can fall to you to find the right solution for both the customer and the firm.

Creating-solutions phrase: "I have had unique situations with customers that have required me to really put on my thinking cap to come up with the right solution."

Creating-solutions phrase: "There are always new problems that can come up that may require new solutions."

Communication Skills

Because the bulk of customer contact is either verbal or through e-mail, excellent communication skills are essential to getting the right customer-service job.

Communication-skills phrases: "My presentations use multimedia to help drive the point home."

Communication-skills phrases: "I make sure to have strong visual components when presenting to make matters clear to everyone."

Communication-skills phrases: "E-mail can be tricky because one-way communication can be ambiguous. I make sure my messages are clear."

Medical and Healthcare Phrases

Medicine is one of the fastest-changing environments today. Those who left the field just a few years ago would be light years behind people who have remained on the cutting edge. Keeping current and maintaining credentials are keys to remaining active in this field.

Keeping Current

Almost everyday there are breakthroughs in medicine. These changes seem to happen faster and faster as time goes on. It is critical to show that you keep up with the latest information in your field.

Keeping-current phrase: "I have been religiously reading [cite name] journal, every month, for the last seven years."

Keeping-current phrase: "With so many breakthroughs, I try to attend as many medical seminars as I can each year."

Credentials

Getting the credentials is just the first step. They need to be current. Always make certain that you do not let them lapse.

It's often easier to maintain an existing credential than renewing one that has lapsed.

Credentials phrase: "All my credentials are current."

Credentials phrase: "Last year I completed the...seminar for credits toward...."

Credentials phrase: "I believe in continuous learning and try to exceed the requirements of maintaining my credentials."

Professionalism

Because people working in the medical field deal with a client's most personal issues, professionalism is key.

Bedside Manner

Patients are often very concerned about issues that may or may not warrant it. In either case, many employers want to know that you will work not just on the patient's physical issues, but also help them with the mental issues that go along with his or her diagnosis (or potential diagnosis).

Bedside-manner phrase: "I care about the entire person, not just their problems and symptoms."

Bedside-manner phrase: "When I work with a patient, I try to explain the entire process in order to reduce their stress and anxiety."

Technical Ability

Knowing how something is done and being able to do it are not always the same. One of the best ways to show that you have the technical ability to perform a task is to tell about your past experience with it. If you don't have that past experience, talk about the similar things you have done and talk about how that would make you able to catch on quickly.

Nonprofit Phrases

This is a very broad field and it is growing every day. There are nonprofit institutions that work for just about every cause imaginable. Each organization or agency, though, has its own unique ideas and philosophies. For this reason, fit within the organization is key. This means more than believing in the cause. It also includes agreeing with the ideals of the individual institution.

Dedication to the Cause

Managers want to see that you believe in the work being done. This is perceived as being important for every employee, from administrative assistants right up to the president and the members of the board. If you can tell why you are interested and believe in the cause, it will go a long way. Many people have interests in specific causes because of their own personal history. This makes a compelling case.

Dedication-to-the-cause phrase: "I have a personal stake in this organization doing well because of my history."

Dedication-to-the-cause phrase: "I want to see this institution thrive because I believe in what we are doing here."

Dedication-to-the-cause phrase: "I will be steadfast in fulfilling any duties assigned to me."

Adaptability

Many nonprofit organizations have fewer resources than necessary. You may need to show that you can do more than one thing. This helps when it comes time for everyone to pitch in, or in cases in which you bring a unique and valuable talent to the group that they wouldn't have without you. Just as a Swiss-Army knife is more than a knife, you too can add value in areas that aren't necessarily in your job description.

Adaptability phrase: "I have a wide variety of skills and I will pitch in where needed."

Adaptability phrase: "I like to learn and will do whatever is necessary for the institution to flourish."

Adaptability phrase: "Think of me as a human 'Swiss-Army knife.'"

Professionalism

Because nonprofits rely on donations from various sources, professionalism is an integral piece of the model. Being professional throughout the interview process will help show you will avoid the type of unprofessional conduct that can embarrass the organization and ultimately put it in jeopardy.

Professionalism phrase: "Maintaining a professional appearance is of the utmost importance to me."

Professionalism phrase: "I always make sure my actions and appearances pass the *'Wall Street Journal* Test.'" (If it appeared in the *Wall Street Journal*, I would be proud.)

Fund-Raising

Although not all jobs in the nonprofit word involve fund-raising, most are in some way or another part of the overall effort. Each employee is responsible for getting the best results possible, which can lead to additional funding. Additionally, many positions are at least tangentially related to the fund-raising effort in some way or another. Show your understanding of the importance of fund-raising and how you will impact the institution in a positive way.

Fund-raising phrase: "I understand that the lifeblood of the agency is its donor base and I, in addition to my job duties, am committed to helping to raise money."

Fund-raising phrase: "I have gained quite a bit of experience with fund-raising through the volunteer organizations I have been affiliated with."

Engineering Phrases

Engineering requires an analytical mind capable of creating real-world solutions using available and appropriate materials. The repercussions of failure can be dire, so great care must go into each project.

Problem-Solving

Each engineering project is a set of problems. Showing that you can come up with the right solution(s) for problems as they come up demonstrates that you will be a valuable member of the team.

Problem-solving phrase: "It's about finding the right solution for the individual project."

Problem-solving phrase: "Although there may be several possible solutions, I feel it's my job to come up with the very best one."

Problem-solving phrase: "I don't consider a problem to be solved until all related issues are put to bed."

Technical Knowledge

This includes schooling, licenses, and other credentials. They should speak for themselves in this field.

Resourcefulness

Solutions to engineering problems are often not obvious at first. A great engineer should be able to use materials in many different ways for a broad array of applications. This includes understanding a material's properties and possibly considering modifications so it can be used for a different application than originally intended. This kind of resourcefulness broadens the number of options at hand.

Cost-Consciousness

For most engineering problems, there can be many solutions. One of the constraints engineers can face is budgets. In business, money is not endless and is almost always an important factor. Employers want to know that you will help find the solutions that work as they are intended to and also make monetary sense.

Cost-consciousness phrase: "Money is always a factor that determines how I go about solving a problem."

Cost-consciousness phrase: "I try to add value by creating a solution that solves the issue and also makes financial sense."

Cost-consciousness phrase: "Working within a given budget is very important to me."

Information-Technology (IT) Phrases

Trouble-Shooting

One of the core skills in the information technology field is the ability to look at a situation, diagnose a problem, and find the right solution. Give examples that showoff your diagnostic abilities.

Trouble-shooting phrase: "Before I try to fix a problem, I make sure that it is correctly diagnosed."

Trouble-shooting phrase: "Sometimes the problem we see is only the tip of the iceberg."

Improvement and Learning

Few fields change as quickly as technology. Although your knowledge today might be cutting-edge and just what the hiring manager needs, his or her needs can and will change quickly. Demonstrating the ability to remain on the cutting edge and adapt rapidly to an ever-changing environments are essential qualities for personnel in this field.

Improvement-and-learning phrase: "It's very important to me to keep on the cutting edge."

Improvement-and-learning phrase: "What kind of training does your firm offer?"

Improvement-and-learning phrase: "I recently completed [cite degree or certification] and I am looking forward to the next phase."

Response Time

IT has become such an integral part of business that issues and problems need immediate attention and fast resolution. Being *good* isn't enough when everything needs to be kept up and running.

Response-time phrase: "Any prolonged period of downtime is totally unacceptable to me."

Response-time phrase: "I understand how critical it is to be up and running. It's my job to make sure things stay that way."

Response-time phrase: "You can count on a very fast response from me whenever issues arise."

Operations Phrases

Independence

Demonstrating that you have the ability to work on your own, make good decisions, and deal with issues as they come up is important, especially in higher-level positions in organizations. Sometimes issues are urgent, and you may be the only one available to make the right decision in the given time frame.

Initiative

Because things can happen quickly and competition is fierce, show that you can take the initiative, whether it is looking for new vendors, finding a more efficient system, or developing an approach that will decrease delivery times.

Time Management

There are only 24 hours in a day, and fewer still in a work day. Much needs to get done, and effective time management is the only way that you can maximize what you and your staff can handle.

Time-management phrase: "Because time is a finite resource, I budget my time carefully."

Time-management phrase: "I use a daily planner to make sure that I get my maximum output from every workday."

Time-management phrase: "I try to anticipate problems and allow time for their solutions to be found in my planning."

Resource Utilization

When an employer is looking at more than one candidate, he or she wants to see what each individual can do with a set of given resources. Show how you can do more with the same, or fewer, resources as others. This will maximize the value you bring to the table.

Leadership and Management Phrases

Being a leader is an art more than a skill. It requires world-class interpersonal and communication skills. It also requires good decision-making, proper management of employees and resources, delegation, and the ability to change as the market does.

Leadership

The ability to lead others, motivate them, and make necessary changes are all important facets of the job. Give evidence of your ability with phrases that show you can lead despite adverse conditions.

Leadership phrase: "I find it to be very satisfying to coach and mentor others."

Leadership phrase: "I bring out the best in others and I help them improve."

Leadership phrase: "Building the right teams can maximize an outcome."

Judgment

One of the challenges managers face is to make good decisions based on the facts they have gathered. Show that you can gather the facts, find problems, make changes, and measure results.

Management

Management is both an art and a science. Each manager has his or her own style. Find out if your management style fits the organization.

Management phrase: "I have a history of excellent coaching and mentoring."

Management phrase: "I have found that people can learn better when they understand the problems and consequences involved."

Management phrase: "I try to set difficult yet attainable goals for my subordinates."

Management phrase: "I believe in giving accurate and helpful feedback so people can continue to grow."

Ability to Motivate Others

Motivating others can be one of the most challenging aspects of management. People are creatures of habit and are often resistant to change. Making speeches isn't going to change much. Be prepared to talk about your methods of motivating your subordinates.

Ability-to-motivate-others phrase: "I strive to develop talent in others."

Ability-to-motivate-others phrase: "I try to find what people are good at and let them do their best work."

Ability-to-motivate-others phrase: "I am passionate about helping others to grow and learn."

Persuasiveness

Managers need to persuade their employees, their peers, and even their superiors in order to be able to succeed.

Delegation

Because each of us has a finite amount of time, energy, and resources, effective delegation becomes essential for effective workflow. Show how you have efficiently delegated tasks to increase your output and performance.

Adaptability

One of the few things we can count on is change. Although most people are resistant to change, managers have to be willing to take the risks in order to reap the rewards. Change is very much a top-down phenomenon.

Adaptability phrase: "Change is one of the only constants we can count on."

Adaptability phrase: "There are always new environments, new factors, and new issues we have to adapt to in order to succeed."

Manufacturing and Production Phrases

This includes the nuts and bolts of production and assembly. There is a constant race to gain better productivity and quality while simultaneously lowering costs. These results can be achieved in a variety of ways.

Improvement

Because manufacturing is usually highly competitive, showing that you can improve processes will make you a more valuable member of the team.

Quality

Quality means different things to different customers. Be sure you understand what quality means to the company you are interviewing with. Once you understand what it values, you can show how you can provide it.

Defect Rate

Low-defect rate means lower costs and better production. Tell how you have decreased the defect rate in the past for your former employers.

Productivity

Because manufacturers usually have high fixed costs, better productivity is critical to increased profit.

Quality Control and Quality Improvement Phrases

Quality control is essential for a firm to have repeat business. Additionally, if quality control is superb, less customer service will be required. Although new quality programs are introduced every year, there are some constants throughout. Quality must be measured, analyzed, and improved.

Details

In order for quality to be up to specifications, even the smallest deviation has to be caught.

Planning

Without proper planning results are almost always unsatisfactory. To show that you have good planning abilities demonstrates that you can get consistent results.

Action

Quality only improves with change. Most people have difficulty with change. Putting ideas into action in the only way change can occur.

Results

You are only as good as the results you can achieve. Make sure you demonstrate your ability and history of getting superior results to others in your field, industry, company, or position.

Administrative Assistant, Administrative, and Support Phrases

Prioritization

The extent to which an employee sets job- and company-related objectives (and action plans to achieve those goals) is an important factor for administrative personnel.

Prioritization phrase: "I am very organized regarding the order in which my work gets done."

Prioritization phrase: "I understand that time is a finite resource, so each task must be prioritized."

Prioritization phrase: "When in a crunch, some things must take priority over others."

Accuracy

Accuracy involves paying attention to the details and accounting for all possibilities, and not letting the small but important items fall to the wayside.

Attendance and Punctuality

This means showing up for work and being ready to start your day ontime, consistently.

Attendance-and-punctuality phrase: "In the last year I only took one sick day."

Attendance-and-punctuality phrase: "I only am absent when it's absolutely unavoidable."

Attendance-and-punctuality phrase: "I'm usually the first in the office in the morning."

Dependability

Dependability deals with the conformance to past practices. Doing things the same way and in a predictable fashion. Showing that you are dependable will help employers understand that you will get consistent results.

Dependability phrase: "You can count on me to deliver."

Dependability phrase: "I have the planning aspect down to a science."

Dependability phrase: "I always plan everything out so that there are no unexpected issues that might delay my ability to deliver on time."

Flexibility

Be willing to pitch in where needed. Another part of flexibility is having the skills to participate in many different types of tasks.

Multitasking

Give examples that show that you have the ability to handle several projects at the same time.

Chapter Worsheet

Prepare yourself with answers to the following:

▶ What are some of the critical areas in your field that you will need to emphasize strengths in?

▶ What phrases will you use to demonstrate these skills?

▶ What questions do you expect to be asked related to this chapter?

▶ What are some possible answers to these questions that position you well?

▶ What other questions might an employer ask about an attribute outside of what was previously outlined for people in your field?

▶ Are you able to use phrases from a different part of the chapter to answer that question effectively?

▶ Are there any additional attributes you want to discuss in order to increase your value to the hiring manager?

The following are a few helpful thoughts on interviewing provided by Dr. Paul Powers, author of *Winning Job Interviews*:

Most people dread job interviewing. They feel it's uncomfortable, it's anxiety-producing, and it requires selling oneself like a product on a supermarket shelf. But it doesn't have to be that way. For example, there are four or five reasons why the psychological dynamics in the interview room are actually in favor of you: the job candidate.

There are a half dozen proven ways to go in to your interview ready to stand head-and-shoulders above your competition. There are almost 20 easy-to-use tools you can use to polish your interviewing skills. There is an easy road map to follow to negotiate the best deal—to get a better salary and/or a better job description.

I've laid them out in *Winning Job Interviews*, and authors like Peter Gray and John Carroll have added to the literature with a host of good, solid, practical ideas to enhance one's personal presentation in any venue. But, and this is a biggie, you, the job candidate, must take ownership of the process.

Researching your targets, understanding your prospects, reading the right books, practicing and polishing your skills, and managing your attitude and stress level are essential elements of any game plan to succeed in today's competitive career world. The days of preparing for an interview by merely getting a good night's sleep and hoping to be "discovered," as a movie starlet from the 1930s, are long gone.

CHAPTER 5

Experience-Level Phrases and Tips for Unusual Circumstances

This chapter is for candidates with unusual circumstances involving the length and type of their work experience or reasons for taking a job. Perhaps you are new to the workforce or you have not been in your position very long. Maybe you fear you are overqualified for the position for which you are applying. Some of you may be returning to the employment scene after a hiatus, or coming out of retirement to work again. Perhaps a downsizing resulted in your position being eliminated. Maybe you were laid off or fired. There may be other factors or extenuating circumstances with which you must contend. What do you do if you are applying for a position for which you have no direct experience yet you have been in the workforce for many years? How do you present yourself when you are just entering the work world?

Included here are typical situations most all of us face sometime during our lifetime. Take note of your current situation and learn how you can shape your search, phrases, responses, networking, and overall marketing effort for maximum results.

Use the tips and phrases to leverage your resume, cover letter, e-mails, and voice mails, and when interviewing.

Entry-Level Job

If you are new to the workforce it is a given, in the interviewer's or employer's mind, that you will not have direct work experience. You are expected to have limited experience. Employers are primarily interested in your potential, attitude, outlook, and ability to learn, adapt, follow directions, think for yourself, communicate orally and in writing, and work with others. They will also be interested in your fundamental job skills—that is, skills and competencies that are needed in most any entry-level position.

Maximize your impact by showing off the skills and attributes you do have. Arrange your resume in a functional basis so these traits are exhibited first, rather than your limited work history. Make sure that you communicate these traits during an interview. Key traits and skills include:

▸ **Computer skills.** List all the software and hardware with which you are proficient. Where known, cite your level of proficiency with the various word processing, spreadsheet, database, and presentation/slide programs. Relay high school and college computer classes that you took and the projects you completed that demonstrate your proficiencies. Full- and part-time work experiences may have required computer applications, as well as college work/study or internships, too.

▸ **Leadership experience.** List past situations where you volunteered or were tapped to serve in leadership roles. What was the situation? What had to be accomplished? What issues did you have to work through to achieve the results, and what were the results in quantitative terms (metrics)?

How long did it take you? How complex was it? How many people were involved? Many of us experienced, firsthand, the challenges of being a leader when we were in high school and/or college. Clubs, organizations, class-office positions, fund-raising and charitable initiatives, churches, temples, and mosques, and so on, all require leaders. What where you involved in? Don't forget summer employment, or those internship experiences.

▶ **Communications skills.** Put forth situations where you had to compile written reports or make oral presentations. Your involvement in the previously-mentioned organizations, along with your classroom work may have also involved communications roles: publicity, stand-up talks, press releases, reports, debates, selling, or persuasive presentations.

▶ **Customer relations and/or selling skills.** Because so many entry-level positions put you in a selling or servicing role (inbound or outbound marketing, call centers, technical help desks, order entry, front counter or on the store floor selling or customer assistance, and so on), you should list experiences that demonstrate your ability to handle customers, work with difficult people or situations, or simply help people make buying decisions. What about your summer, holiday, or after-school jobs? Any of them involve duties that put you in front of people? Selling? On the phone?

▶ **Foreign language fluency.** Fluency in a foreign language, especially Spanish or Chinese, is a real asset. More and more positions require multilingual language skills. Your knowledge of second (or third!) language puts you ahead of the line when looking for that first real, full-time job. Describe your competencies (beginner, intermediate, advanced, or expert) in each of the following: reading, writing, and speaking. If your personal or educational journeys have included traveling, studying, or working in a foreign land, make note of such.

Because you are a newcomer to the workforce, put focus on what you learned from your experiences, as well as what you accomplished. Employers want to see or hear that you have the ability to learn and grow. They are less concerned with what you know and more interested in what you can become. This has a lot to do with your attitude, and how you portray your experiences.

A positive attitude, eagerness to learn, and the right phrases go a very long way. Avoid bullet points that tell the more obvious. For example, experience working for a gas station might not seem to be apropos to the business world, but the following example illustrates how you can demonstrate relevance to a potential employer.

Poor Phrasing

▸ Responsible for pumping gasoline.
▸ Checked customers' fluid levels and topped off as necessary.
▸ Handled cash and credit card transactions.

Good Phrasing

▸ Provided prompt, courteous service to station customers.
▸ Educated customers on preventative maintenance tips and increased supply sales by 15 percent with cross-selling techniques.
▸ Generated business leads through word-of-mouth marketing and testimonials.
▸ Trusted to work alone with large cash transactions.
▸ Exceeded customer-satisfaction expectations as measured by company surveys.

New Positions

Occasionally you will get wind of a position that is newly created. It hadn't existed before but, due to restructuring, growth, talent voids, and so on, an organization has created a position with new, modified, or combined responsibilities. They have attempted to define the new job, its duties and responsibilities, resources available, the scope of interaction with other professionals, and, most importantly, the end result of the position (that is, what the job is to do and why). The job surfaced because a need was not being met internally. You believe you can meet that need!

Newly created positions are often of the most difficult to land. Unlike a long-standing position where the job responsibilities and candidate specifications have been time-tested, new positions are "works in progress." Management thinks they know what they need, but they often have conflicting views. There may not be total agreement on what the company really wants, what duties this new position will have, and what experience and skills they are looking for in the candidates for the position. They may not know exactly where to source candidates. Each management member may be trying to accomplish different goals through the addition of this position.

To make matters even more complicated, each person on the interview team may evaluate candidates in a totally different way. They each may have different beliefs about what makes for a fit between a candidate and the job. Add in the different interviewing styles and what we have is a big mess. How do you please several different people who may be looking for different things? How do you know what they are seeking in the first place? Will you be trying to hit a moving target when applying or interviewing?

Although the hiring manager is typically the final decision-maker in most interview situations, a newly created position requires consensus hiring. Each party involved in the interviewing process could be very influential because he or she has a different perspective of the position. The hiring manager's boss, if involved in the interviews, is a very pivotal player who may have a different agenda. Rather than quickly verifying that the manager's choice is satisfactory, this person will be much more involved in the hiring decision, or be the sole decision-maker of who is hired.

When you do interview, be prepared to be flexible. Listen carefully to the members of the interview team for their view of the position. Where conflicting views are expressed openly mention that you understand the value of all perspectives. Ask for clarification from each of the people you interview. Your job is to find the common thread, the areas that all agree are important, and demonstrate how you are uniquely qualified to do that work. Make sure you ask many questions that help clarify the position responsibilities. Offer suggestions as to what might be needed. Often new positions are shaped around the unique offerings of a candidate such as yourself, so you need to demonstrate your flexibility in new work situations. Offer examples of times when you were assigned work that was not clear. What did you do to better define the expectations? What did you personally do? What did you have to learn? What skills did you have to acquire to do the project? What were the results? What did you learn along the way? How would you apply this experience or process to this new job?

Don't hesitate to ask the interviewers or hiring manager what he or she sees in you or your resume that is appealing with respect to the new position. Take that information and expand upon those strengths. Be bold and also ask what concerns they might have. Calmly overcome those objections by bringing new information to their attention that illustrates you have experience (and results) in those areas. If you do not possess such, then relay past situations where you didn't have the requisite experience or know-how but, because of your drive and ability to learn new things, you successfully took on the challenge.

As mentioned earlier, the management team interviewing you may not be totally clear on the job and candidate definitions, so make liberal use of clarification questions, rephrasing or restating what the interviewer said, and summarizing the job. All this will result in new or added information about the job. The more information you have the better you can demonstrate that you are right for the position, and perhaps the only person for the job. If you can create this uniqueness you will have leverage with the terms of the job offer.

Lateral or Downward Moves

Let's take a look at the reasons a person might have interest in taking another job with similar or less duties and compensation. There can be a multitude of reasons (and all legitimate), but you have to be prepared to sell the hiring company on the reasons why. For recruiters, companies, and hiring managers, it seems counter-intuitive for a person to not want to advance. This can be a very difficult sell to a potential employer. Let's take a look at some of the reasons you may seek a change and be willing to take a lateral move (no improvement in pay) or a step back (work for less than you do now):

- ▶ Work/life balance.
- ▶ Shorter commute.
- ▶ Better or different hours.
- ▶ No future with current company.
- ▶ Company on the decline.
- ▶ Dislike your boss.
- ▶ Dislike your job.
- ▶ Tuition reimbursement.
- ▶ Fits in with long-term career development strategy.
- ▶ Want to return to a prior role.
- ▶ Desire to change industries.

▸ Better benefits and/or less costly.

▸ More liberal vacation and holiday policy.

▸ Don't like the culture.

▸ Don't like the pressure.

▸ Childcare facilities.

▸ Made a bad decision.

▸ Was misled.

▸ Not appreciated.

These, and other circumstances not listed, can be put in two distinct groups, the first being extrinsic reasons for changing, and the other being intrinsic. Extrinsic reasons have little or nothing to do with the current company and more to do with the new company and job you seek. Better location or commute, flexible hours, and desirable industry or work experience, for example. Intrinsic reasons are just the reverse. They have little to do with the new company and everything to do with the current. Intrinsic reasons involve some negative with your current employer.

When answering the question "Why do you want to come to work here (for the same money)?" you want your answer to always be positive. If your rational is extrinsic, it is normally an easy sell and accepted on its face value. In intrinsic circumstances you want to shift the discussion away from the negatives of your current job, company, or boss to the positives of the new employer. Avoid the negatives. Interviewers and hiring managers all too often hear applicants bad mouth their current employer and speak disparagingly about their work responsibilities and boss. In short, they don't want whiners in their organization. So when you talk about your employer or job or boss in even in the slightest negative connotation, you may cast yourself as another one of those whiners.

The reality is that if the negative situation did not exist or had been turned around, you most likely would be staying with the organization. Because it hasn't, you have decided to leave (run away from?) the company. Talking about the negatives can put you on a slippery slope. The more you say the more difficult it becomes to land the job. A brief and simple statement will suffice. If silence follows your "confession" do not be tempted to jump in and explain it further. In most circumstances your explanation will satisfy the interviewer. As with the "don't ask, don't tell" scenario (presented in Chapter 6), interviewers are often relieved that they don't have to push for additional information. However, if you blurt out too much then the interviewer is obligated to explore your circumstance to the fullest possible extent.

Think about the following combinations of phrases to use as a response to the question "Why do you want to join our company?" (In brackets are the real reasons for changing jobs.)

- ▸ "It is not often that one can take on a challenging job and have it be minutes from home." [too long of a commute]

- ▸ "As much as I like my current employer and boss I seen more opportunities to grow and advance here as you are in a leading-edge technology organization." [current company lagging the market]

- ▸ "With your on-site childcare facility I can better focus on my job and work overtime, when necessary." [problem with present employer regarding overtime and absences due to child needs]

- ▸ "I noticed in last week's Sunday business section your CEO was quoted saying that eMarketing will be the thrust for next year. I have training in that area and would like to see more of my work be devoted to that arena." [under-utilized and under-appreciated in present job]

- ▸ "With your flexible shift hours I will avoid having to drive during rush-hour periods and I will be less stressed and more productive for you."

[work/life balance out of sync or having problems in current job]

▶ "I have come to learn that I am most productive and happiest when I am in an individual contributor role as opposed to supervising others in their work. This position would allow me to return to creative design work." [hired or promoted into a supervisory or managerial role and does not enjoy it]

▶ "As you read in the papers and heard on the news, my company is experiencing financial problems and possibly facing bankruptcy. Were it not for that, I would not be here interviewing. It is not that I dislike the hard work that goes with turning around a company, but my circumstances have changed since joining them. I am now married and have two young children." [company in trouble, but doesn't want to appear to be someone who jumps ship when the going gets tough as the new employer will have doubts should it, too, experience difficult times]

▶ "Throughout my entire career I have worked for a number of bosses. Some were a delight to work with; others were not. But I had respect for all of them. That changed last year. I regard your firm as one that values its employees and expects the same from its supervisors." [bad boss situation that shouldn't be discussed further]

▶ "I seek an organization that places greater importance on people working as a team." [current company not team-oriented and employees do not get along; it may be very cutthroat or competitive]

▶ "I miss the excitement of a customer-oriented firm. I have always thrived in that kind of environment." [current employer not customer-focused]

▸ "My employer is relocating its technical center to another state. I have moved my family several times in the past but this time it is not appropriate." [Company or job relocations are an everyday event and companies understand such personal decisions. However, do not make such a statement if you were not extended an offer to relocate.]

▸ "The firm was acquired by a west coast firm and the east cost operation is being closed. Only a small number of people have been asked to relocate. I can understand the rationale for such. I see an opportunity in all this, and that is to cross over to the nonprofit sector, where my true interests are." [a way to divert the discussion away from not being asked, for performance reasons, to relocate]

▸ "The business went through a major reorganization and my position, along with a significant number of other jobs in our division, was eliminated. It was anticipated and, although my work was highly valued, they are closing down my department." [as with the relocation example, keeps the discussion away from why your company may have targeted your job]

There is value in combining two or more phrases as your response. It relays that you have put a lot of thought into why you want to make the job change. It is not for "selfish" gain, but rather for reasons that also benefit the employer. Although employers acknowledge that there can be personal reasons for leaving your present company and pursuing them, they really would like to know that you have a keen interest in the job and are committed to the making a difference in its organization. Give them those reasons and they will be less interested in the "intrinsic" items around your wanting to leave your current employer.

When You Are Significantly Overqualified for the Position

Although your reasons, extrinsically or intrinsically motivated, for pursuing a job for which you are more than qualified may be rational and reasonable to you, the employer may have preconceived notions about overqualified applicants. These subjective beliefs and thoughts include:

▸ You may be bored in the job.

▸ You will leave within a short period of time.

▸ You are desperate and will take anything just to be employed.

▸ You will use the job and company as leverage for your next job outside the company.

▸ You will be a threat to your boss.

▸ You will be a "know-it-all" and tell people how to do their jobs or run the department.

Rarely are these thoughts put in the form of a question. Whether explicitly expressed or implicitly reflected in thought, your goal is to overcome these objections. Perhaps you have been in this situation before. If so, share how you quickly integrated into the department, performed your work well, and stayed within your boundaries. Another approach would be to keep the interview focused on the extrinsic reasons for pursuing the job and why you view it as a viable tradeoff. Emphasize that you bring solid experience and know-how that can be immediately utilized (at the company's salary rate for the position) and you obtain work/life elements (see earlier list of reasons for taking a "lesser" job), which are "priceless."

What if You Have Been Fired From a Company?

Being fired has a stigma attached to it. It hurts people's self-confidence as well as their ability to gain employment. Most interviewers assume that you did something so egregious that you deserved to be fired. Yet there can be a multitude of logical reasons why you lost your job. You will be asked to explain the situation and you need to be straightforward and honest in your answer. Your objective is to defuse the situation by providing a rational explanation. Unless the circumstances surrounding your termination dealt with illegal or inappropriate behavior you should be able to set forth what prompted the termination, what led up to it, and what you have learned from it.

In recent years the services of an outplacement or job transition firm have been made available to the fired or terminated employee. There are several reasons why. First, the cost of such counseling has declined significantly while the content of the services has increased multifold. The second reason is more of an altruistic one. Bad things happen to well-intended people. You may have erred in your job. The company may have made some mistakes, too. Regardless, a change was necessary and both parties need to move on. One way of helping you is to extend outplacement counseling, not only to help you find new employment, but to understand what precipitated the firing and remedy those shortcomings. Be attentive to using suggested phrasings of why you were terminated. They are professionals in this arena and know how to best position the "parting of ways."

Often individuals in this situation may hedge (fudge?) a bit on telling the interviewer why he or she is no longer with the company by stating, "I received a package," or "They extended me a package." The hope here is that the interviewer takes that as meaning that the person was laid off or part of a major downsizing, reorganization, or relocation. But what if the interviewer follows up with questions such as, "How many, in total, were affected by this?", "I never saw anything in the press about this; tell me more.", or "Whom can I contact to confirm this workforce change?" Now you are in a situation of being less than straightforward, and the interviewer will now become a "hunter" looking for reasons to not hire you, rather than reasons to hire you.

In a similar vein, companies sometimes give you the option to resign. The authors have mixed thoughts on whether it is beneficial or not. Although it may seem less detrimental to say you resigned, you still have to explain why! Even if armed with the best phrases to deflect focus on what really happened, your "story" usually unravels when the interviewer asks follow-up questions such as, "Were you fired or going to be fired?" If you answer yes it still begs the question of why. If you respond no then you will be asked, "If you had not resigned would you still have your job?", "Wouldn't it have been better to continue working while looking for a new job?", or "Why would you just quit and walk away from your job?" You just left yourself open for significant probing from the interviewer and closed the door on being considered for the position.

So what do you say? As stated, if you are receiving job-placement counseling, then follow the counselor's specific advice. In general they (and we) recommend that you be straightforward, truthful, and reflective. Your phrasings should be thought out ahead of time, scripted, and rehearsed. By *reflective* we mean that you offer some personal perspective on the situation (Why did you find yourself in the circumstances? What you have learned from it? How you will apply that learning in the future with your next employer). You may be surprised to see the interviewer accept these truths and move on to gaining insight into your skills, experiences, and future interests. After all, job mismatches and performance misses do happen, and for a variety of reasons—some the employee's doing and others the company's fault.

Many interviewers are accepting of a simple, truthful statement on your behalf. In many ways they don't want to go beyond what you state. It is when you are hesitant, wordy, evasive, or silent that he or she begins to think there is more than meets the eye with your explanation. What concerns interviewers and HR departments are:

▸ Violation of company rules.

▸ Falsification of records.

▸ Poor attendance or attitude.

▸ Illegal acts.

▸ Insubordination.

▸ Embezzlement.

▸ Acts of harassment.

▸ Incompetence.

The following are samples of phrasings to use when explaining why you were terminated.

When you script your explanation also enlist the cooperation of your reference(s). As mentioned, the interviewing company is primarily interested in the validity and integrity of your statement and, when confirmed by your reference(s), it brings positive closure on that issue.

▸ "I left the company to devote my full efforts in locating a position and company that is a better fit with my skills and interests. I might have made a mistake in taking this position two years ago, as I was led to believe I would be managing the work of others but I am not. And instead I am doing programming work. I did not think it fair to myself and the company to try to look for new opportunities while still working there."

▶ "I knew going into this position that my brief tenure as a manager with my former company may not have been adequate preparation for this department-head position and that proved true! I was not accustomed to managing such a large group. My 360-degree evaluations reflected that I was respected for my technical know-how, but that my team felt micro-managed. It really was not fair to them and it caused long, unnecessary work hours for me. I learned a lot from the experience and from my boss. I also sought out a close friend and mentor for advice. I now better know my strengths [cite] and my limitations. More importantly, I know what I am best fit for [talk about the interviewer's company and position opening]."

▶ "I experienced a number of absences that reflected poorly on my attendance record. Ultimately I exceeded the number allowed by company policy and I was terminated. I never had difficulty doing the work, just difficulty being at work. My employer will confirm that for you. The absences were highly personal and, after losing my job, I sought professional help that remedied things. You are welcome to contact that person also." [A future employer's prime concern is that whatever prompted you to be terminated will not happen again in the future. Offering confirmation of the situation(s) also lowers or eliminates the interviewer's anxiety.]

▶ "Looking back on this I see that I underestimated the time it would take to complete the project. Earlier projects had been completed on time, on budget, and to the requirements, but this one missed the mark. It was my first project involving an international team and I learned, albeit too late, that my section leaders overseas had different priorities. My boss had no choice but to make a staffing change. I now see what I could have done [elborate what you learned and how you would do it differently the next time]."

▸ "I have had a number of bosses throughout the years and most of them had less technical know-how than I. They were astute enough to make use my experience and we all not only looked good, but we delivered results. They, for the most part, were open to my suggestions. My last manager, however, came from the outside, seemed uncomfortable in the role, and seemed threatened by my knowledge and status in the company. I could see the writing on the wall. I had already been looking for other work before my job was eliminated. I am okay with it as my work interests have shifted during the past several years." [Sometimes life deals you a bad hand and you deal with it. This approach minimizes additional questions on the interviewer's behalf.]

Learn, live, explain, and move on. Companies take risks with employees all the time and will be willing to take a chance on someone who was fired from his or her job. It is all about the nature of the risk and being able to manage it. At all levels, it is about performance, results, and politics, or a mix of each. Someone can fail in one job, but be highly successful in the next. The interviewer's objective is to obtain a clear understanding of what and why something happened, whether it could happen again, and, if not, then to focus on the items of real meaning (that is, your education, training, experiences, accomplishments, work and management style, and so on). If your phrasings help the interviewer move towards, rather than away, from that goal, then you will find yourself in a new job.

Landing That Promotion

After being in a position for a while, many things come as second nature. At some point it is natural to seek upward mobility in your company and the company, most likely, is thinking along the same lines. Assuming you have enough experience, the right skills, are a good match for the corporate culture of the firm, are well thought of and liked by those above and around you, and have either avoided company politics or played the game correctly, you have an excellent chance of moving up when the time is right (or even before). Interviewing internally for a position that will be a promotion for you is somewhat similar to going after a bigger position in another company. You have to demonstrate that you have the ability and motivation to perform the new job. However, when pursuing an internal advancement you are not an unknown quantity. That can be good or bad for you! Your past and present job performance is known, as well as your work and communications style. It may indicate that you are more than ready for a new assignment, that it may be a stretch but that it is worth a go, or that you are not quite ready (or may never be ready) for a promotion.

You should approach a promotional job interview the same way you would interviewing for a new job on the outside. Do your homework on the job, the duties and responsibilities, the skills and experiences needed, the resources available to you to be successful, your boss and peers, and so on. Get your hands on the official job description. Seek out past or current incumbents of that job or similar jobs. People who have worked for and with the manager for whom you will be working. What is it about? What are the demands? What are the tough elements? What is the upside (and downside) of taking the position?

What skills and abilities are needed to successfully perform the new job? Do you have those skills? Are you capable of (or interested in) acquiring the skills and know-how? Are you pursuing the right job, and for the right reason? High performers are often sought out for promotions, but sometimes for the wrong reasons. Many organizations fall victim to the philosophy of "SuperWorker equals SuperVisor." They promote someone who may not have the supervisory, managerial, or leadership skills needed in the new job. Other skills and experiences may be lacking or minimal, such as: project management, communications and presentation, budgeting and planning, and so on. The end result is that someone may take on a job that he or she is not capable of handling, or he or she may be unhappy with the new role. Similarly, the company now has to find a replacement for one of its best individual performers. This "superperson" phenomenon happens quite frequently in the sales arena. Companies, without thinking it through, often promote their best salesperson to become the sales manager. Not the best of moves for either the company or the individual if the person is not equipped to be a manager, or if he or she is best suited for selling.

So, it is in the best interest of the company, the manager, and the employee pursuing the promotion to be confident that the he or she is qualified to do the job or has the ability to acquire the skills on the job. The employee needs to demonstrate the same during internal interviews. For example:

> ▸ "I have accomplished a lot over the past two years and these achievements have prepared me for this position. For example...." [Link your accomplishments to the expectations of the new job. Where there is not a direct correlation then illustrate work processes and results that parallel what is expected in the new job.]

> ▸ "I realize that certain elements of this job will be new to me, and the same situation surfaced three years ago, when I stepped into my current role. I was able to acquire the requisite know-how in a

short period of time." [This is one way to demonstrate that you have the ability to take on new skill and knowledge areas.]

▸ "Human Resources shared with me the description for this management position. I reviewed each of the duties and responsibilities and was pleased to see that I have successfully done similar work, albeit on a smaller scale, in the job I currently hold." [Take the initiative to review the job description and to map the individual "bullets" to specific work responsibilities and achievements with your current position. Don't forget to include metrics.]

▸ "Sharon Thompson, the prior incumbent in this position, encouraged me to help out during peak-work periods. I learned a lot from her and the experiences. One of the 'take-aways' from the experience was...." [If you indeed had an opportunity to help out or fill in for the incumbent during a vacation period, a leave of absence, or when the position was vacant then make sure you share what you did and the results.]

▸ "From a distance I have watched this department and the challenges the manager faces. I have a couple of important observations and suggestions on how to improve the work flow." [Wherever possible, offer up insight and solutions. Even better is to relay past situations where you have encountered similar circumstances. What were they? What did you do? What were the results?]

▸ "Rather than make a decision right this moment, what if I were to take on some of the responsibilities in an interim capacity so that the work gets done without further delays and you have the opportunity to see my approach to work?"

Preparing for the Promotional Interview

Review your work history and accomplishments during your tenure with the company. Utilize the summary technique outlined earlier in the book; state the situation or problem, what was expected, what you did, how you did it, and the end results in measurable terms. Refresh yourself on your work history and accomplishments prior to joining the organization. There may be some experiences and skills you acquired that are directly related to the new position. Most importantly, prepare yourself with answers to the following questions:

▸ "What appeals to you about this position? Why do you want it?" [Link it to your long-term career plans or goals, mention that you are prepared for it, and explain that it represents work that will be highly gratifying and challenging to you.]

▸ "What are your long-term job or career aspirations?" [Keep it in the company—that is, talk about where ultimately you want to be in the company, not external objectives.]

▸ "What is your current job?", "What do you do?", "Why is it important?", or "How does it relate to this position?" [You are in the best position to highlight the key elements of your current position and it is preparing you for this one.]

▸ "Tell me your understanding of the position?" [This is your chance to demonstrate that you know the content of the position and explain the important role it plays in the overall scheme of things.]

▸ "What would you bring to the job?", or "What qualifies you for this position?" [Recite the skills, experience, and know-how you can apply to the job. Make direct, one-to-one matching of each requirement and specific elements of your background.]

▸ "What are your strengths?" [In addition to reiterating your strong suits as related to the position, also introduce a characteristic, skill, or behavioral trait that makes you unique. Highlight something that the interviewer(s) would not have thought about.]

▸ "What are your weaknesses?", "What areas do you need to improve?", or "What are your shortcomings?" [These questions were covered in an earlier chapter. Your best response is either: (a) something unrelated or minor to the job (for example, your word-processing skills) or (b) a skill or knowledge point that can be readily rectified, once on the job, through coaching, reading, orientation, a short training course, and so on.]

▸ "What changes would you make to or in the job?", "Why?", or "How would you go about accomplishing them?" [This is your opportunity to shine. Highlight two or three initiatives. Just make sure that the organization wants changes.]

▸ "If not you, then who else in the organization is right for this job?" [Interesting question! If you feel you are the only one qualified, state such and back it up with solid reasons why. Don't be negative about other possible candidates. Alternatively, there may be others who are equally or better qualified. Your answer should be complimentary of the other individuals, as it will be a positive sign of how you value talent.]

Other questions that might be asked:

▸ "Can you describe your management style?"

▸ "What makes for a successful leader?" or "What kind of leader are you?"

▸ "Tell me about a problem you had in the past with one of your employees?", "What was it?",

"How did it affect the department?", or "How did you address it?"

▶ "What do you enjoy most about your current position?" or "What do you enjoy least?"

▶ "What is your greatest accomplishment?", "What was the biggest mistake you have made?", and "What did you learn from it?"

▶ "When asked, what would your current boss say about you? Your work colleagues?"

▶ "How have you been preparing yourself for this promotion?"

▶ "What have been your educational pursuits in support of this job?"

Also remember that much can be learned about you not only by how you answer the questions in the interview, but by what questions you ask the interviewer and/or hiring manager. Your questions will reveal much about you: what you think about, how you assimilate and process information, what makes you "tick," and so on. The responses you receive will, in turn, provide you with critical facts about the job that you can then restate or reframe for your own situation to illustrate your qualifications. What might be some insightful questions?

▶ "What is the most critical component of this position? What is the most difficult part?"

▶ "What short-term actions and changes might be necessary?"

▶ "What expectations do you have of the next incumbent?"

▶ "How will the selection decision be made?"

▶ "What strengths do you believe I would bring to the position?"

▶ "Where might my background be light? What concerns, if any, would you have about my candidacy?"

▶ "What things would you do to make sure I succeed in the job?"

▶ "What would be the 30-, 90-, and 120-day goals for the position? What would you expect to be accomplished in the first year?"

▶ "The prior incumbent, what were his or her strengths? Weaknesses? How did this affect the position?"

▶ "Tell me about the people working for this position. Key players or stars? Performance issues?"

▶ "What is the budget I have to work with?"

▶ "What is your management style? Describe yourself."

Catch-22 Situations

There will be many a time when you pursue a position for which you believe your are qualified, yet the door is closed to you because:

▶ You don't have enough experience.

▶ Your experience is in the wrong field.

▶ Your experience is in the wrong industry or business.

In any of these situations, the company's response is to come back when you have the requisite experience. The frustration, of course, is how to secure such experience if they, or similar companies, will not hire you. It is a classic "catch-22" situation. So how do you overcome the companies' objections and convince them you can do or learn the job? Here are some tips:

1. Do your homework and anticipate their objections. Research the job, the company, and the industry or business sector. Why is it supposedly different? What common threads exist with your background? (Do this before you even apply for the position or go for an interview.)

2. Work on framing phrases around these common denominators—how you do things in your current job, and how a similar approach or process will work in the job for which you are applying.

3. If you are lacking the requisite years of experience, make note of what you have accomplished in such a short time, and what you have learned. Focus on the end result (what was accomplished and how you did it), and attach metrics to both (time, output, percent of improvement, reduced errors, and so on).

4. If your experience is in an unrelated industry or business don't make the claim that "it is all the same," because it isn't. No two jobs, companies, or industries are the same, but there can be parallels to each other. Look for those areas, processes, work approaches, and analytical or problem-solving approaches that can be successfully applied in both spaces. Here are organizational categories that seem to be the most disparate and most difficult to cross over from one to another:

   ▶ Healthcare.
   ▶ Government.
   ▶ Nonprofit.
   ▶ Retail.
   ▶ Manufacturing.
   ▶ Military.
   ▶ Banking or financial services.
   ▶ eBusiness or Internet-based companies.

Biases exist within each sector about the ability of someone coming out of one of the other sectors. Yet stories abound about individuals who "crossed over" and, by applying core work/organizational principles or being flexible in the approach, succeeded.

Find those common elements and you will have a greater probability of landing the job.

5. Capture your successes of the past. Identify earlier times when you were faced with a new task, job, company, or industry and you applied these "basics" with positive results.

6. Address the parallels up front in your cover letter, telephone call, e-mail, or however you plan on gaining someone's attention and securing an interview. Most individuals ignore this important tip when initially communicating about the job and, sadly, their resumes do not make it to the "to-call" pile.

7. When interviewing, ask the hiring manager how others without the requisite job or industry/business experience succeeded in this company. Demonstrate that you are capable of doing the same.

Chapter Worksheet

▸ What is your current situation? Job? Company? Skills, knowledge, and experience? Positives? Negatives?

▸ What is the position and company where you seek employment? Skills, knowledge, and experience required? Positives? Negatives? Why do you want the position?

▸ What are the major differences in the jobs? In your experience? In industries? What obstacles do you anticipate to getting the job? How will they perceive you? How do you plan on overcoming or bridging those differences?

▸ What are the major similarities? What job skills and processes are the same? How might, or must, you adapt in order to be successful? Have you done such before? How will you communicate all this?

▸ What questions will you most likely be asked during an interview, and what are your answers?

▸ What questions should you ask your interviewers?

CHAPTER 6

Personal Attributes

Don't Ask...Don't Tell

Without fail, the most difficult decision you have when interviewing, networking, or constructing your resume is whether to include personal attributes and circumstances. In many respects things about your personal life are exactly that: personal. Mentioning personal situations or responding to personal questions may cast a negative light on your candidacy. Not knowing the attitudes of the other party, nor the reason for asking a personal question, one's stance should be to not disclose such information. So what is one to do when the "don't ask, don't tell" rule is broken? Worse yet, what is one to do when the question borders on being illegal, inappropriate, or not relevant to the position and your ability to perform the job?

Let's discuss those situations where the interviewer asks illegal questions of and about you. Most hiring managers have been drilled and drilled on the "do's" and "don'ts" of interviewing and adhere to strict guidelines. They know not to ask

questions about race, sex, sexual preference, religion, nation-
ality, marital status, and so on. Not only do they know not to
ask about these and other items, such as number and ages of
children, type of car owned, hobbies, and personal interests,
but they also know that such questions are simply not job-
related. Still, there are some who are counseled not to ask
such questions but still do, and then there will be people who
haven't the faintest clue and insist on asking inappropriate
and illegal questions. How do you handle these kinds of people?

First, when you experience such questions, you have to
immediately decide if this is a person and a company for whom
you want to work. The fact that you are being asked illegal
questions says a lot about the individual and the company.
The odds are that you would not enjoy working there. In such
instances your response might be, "Excuse me, I do not see
what this question has to do with the position and my being
qualified," "I believe that your question is illegal to ask," or
"Would you explain what this question has to do with the position and my candidacy?" Because you have already decided
that you have no further interest in this company and the
position you can say whatever you want. It is quite possible
that you have been discriminated against and have the option of pursuing legal action. Only your attorney can advise
you about that.

There are, however, rare circumstances where the exist-
ence of such an inappropriate question does not mean the
person or company is bad. Perhaps the person is naïve in his
or her interviewing know-how, perhaps nervous, or ignorant.
In such a situation you might say, "Do you really mean to ask
that question, as it is illegal and I don't intend to answer it?",
or "How about we discuss my most recent work experiences
so you have a better idea of my qualifications?" Take the lead,
change the subject, and move on. The odds are that the interviewer will be relieved that you did not make a big issue over
the error.

In any of these situations you will want to alert your Human Resources department contact, the person hosting your interview visit, that you were asked illegal or inappropriate questions; "I just wanted to let you know that the hiring manager, in his interview with me, put forth questions which were not really relevant to the job and my qualifications," "I was offended by the questions," or "I sense he (or she) did it unintentionally. I am really interested in the position and would like to believe it was just an error."

Dumb Questions…Smart Answers

Rarely today does one experience illegal or inappropriate questions, but be prepared for the plethora of dumb questions relating to you, your work experiences, and your personal circumstances. Some are acceptable rewordings of illegal questions, and others are "pet" questions of the interviewer or questions put forth to take the insecurity out of the hiring decision. Here are some examples:

Question(s): "Is there anything or any reason that would prevent you from being at work on time?" Because an interviewer cannot ask, "Do you have children?", "Who sees your child off to school?", or "What kind of car do you own?", he or she will try to determine the reliability of your transportation by turning the question around.

Answer by saying no. This normally satisfies the individual. Alternatively, you could volunteer information that puts to rest the interviewer's insecurity: "Are you asking if I have reliable transportation? Yes, I do", or "I am a very early riser and have never been late for work."

Question(s): "You have far too much experience for this position," or, "You are overqualified for this job." This could be interpreted as implying you are too old for the position in the eyes of the interviewer, or it could be a statement to eventually get around to the fact the company cannot pay what your experience commands. It could even be that the manager is concerned that you will not stay long in the job, opting for something better the minute it surfaces.

Turn the length of experience into a positive for the hiring manager. "That should make you feel good because I will need little or no training and certainly can work with minimal supervision, giving you more time for you work," or "My previous employer raised that same question but over the three years I worked there they came to appreciate the fact that I brought added value."

Turn the dumb question into a smart answer, an answer that prompts the listener to say, "Oh, I hadn't thought of that!" Use the dumb question as an opportunity to provide useful information that might otherwise never come out in an interview.

Another tactic with dumb questions or statements is to respond with your own question. The TV show *Whose Line Is It Anyway?* had a fun segment where a question always follows a question in a conversation. There are many general responsive questions you could use:

Statement/Question: "You have too much experience."

Answer: "Wouldn't you want a highly qualified person in this position?

Statement/Question: "We had an older, more experienced person in mind."

Answer: "What would you consider to be the minimal experience? What competencies do you require?"

Statement/Question: "Is there anything that would prevent you from working overtime?"

Answer: "Could you give me an example of a typical overtime situation or schedule?

Let's Not Get Too Personal!

How many times have you seen personal information at the end of a resume? Statements such as:

"Married with two teen daughters. Avid golfer. Member of Saint Anthony's Church. Staff Volunteer with Smith for Congress Campaign. Speak and write Polish."

Or

"Single parent. Part-time personal trainer, triathlete, and mountain climber. Black belt in karate."

Or

"Recently remarried. Two adult children. Enjoy competitive ballroom dancing and exhibitions. Member of Shalom Temple Men's Choir."

Although everyone is different and proud of his or her family circumstances and personal achievements, the authors recommend that you not put any personal highlights at the end of your resume. Why? There are two very good reasons why all this should be left off. First, from a utility standpoint, the comments, along with the "personal" header, take up valuable space that can be used for job-related accomplishments. Think about the times you tweak the margins, decrease the font size, or abbreviate words in order to find more space to say one or two more items relating to your work accomplishments. Now the resume requires drug-store reading glasses in order to read it, and it is so compressed that key elements do not stand out. Eliminating personal attributes frees space without having to resort to desperate tactics.

The second and more important reason to not put personal information on the resume is that it is personal! You may view the personal statement or accomplishment as admirable but the reader may see it differently. People have their own perceptions, values, and, yes, their own set of biases. You do not know how someone will react to your personal statement. With all the right credentials and experience for the position opening you certainly would not want to jeopardize your candidacy. Similar to the previous "don't ask...don't tell" advice, you will find that most interviewers will not ask personal questions. And you, in turn, should not volunteer.

Of course, there is an exception to every rule and the exception for resumes and cover letters is to put down certain bits of personal information only when you know it is safe and compatible with the hiring manager and company climate. For example, you know that the company and its employees are very involved in, let's say, AmeriCares. You are also a volunteer for AmeriCares. In such a case, by all means include this in either your cover letter or in the resume:

> "For many years I have been a volunteer with the local AmeriCares organization and have met a number of ABC's employees, including Larry Hines and Marsha Latterly. They speak highly of ABC as a career-oriented employer."

> Or

> "I was recently volunteering with Bill Foster at a local AmeriCares weekend project. He mentioned that ABC is seeking a Senior Financial Analyst and that I should contact you."

With some research on the company, reading of annual reports and other literature, and by contacting people in your network who know of or work(ed) for the company, you can ascertain those important bits of information. Never make yourself out to be something you aren't, but if there is a match in your personal life with the endeavors or traits of the company and its employees you should take advantage of that. So, if you are applying to a nonprofit, charitable agency and you have volunteered in other organizations, include that information.

Still, some of your personal "matches" with the company and the people you interview may not be appropriate to put down on paper, but certainly warrant verbal mention during select interviews. Again, by doing a thorough job of researching and networking, you may turn up elements of compatibility. So if golfing is something you and the interviewer have in common, work it in. Next you will learn how to make this small talk into big results.

Good Questions...Great Answers!
How to Leverage Your
Personal Attributes and Accomplishments

You will frequently come upon interviewers who are well-versed in behavioral interviewing. The script usually goes as follows:

> "Tell me about a time when you were asked to be a team leader on a project that you had limited or no past experience. What was it? How did you approach it, and what was the final outcome?"

Or

> "Have you ever been placed in a situation where the subject was foreign to you, yet you were expected to manage the activity? How did you approach it? What did you accomplish?"

Well, when faced with good questions such as these, give them great answers! Perhaps it is a past work situation or, even better, a page from your personal life. How about the time you were asked to lead your church's weekend family camping retreat? Or the occasion where you were the community chairperson for the interagency Thanksgiving food drive? Remember when you were the logistics head for the Community Chorale's Southern U.S. concert tour? These are opportunities to illustrate your versatility, drive, leadership, and positive results. Now you have turned a neutral-sounding personal attribute into a very impressive accomplishment. The know-how, tools, PC software, communications, leadership traits, and so on, that you utilized are the very same power skills you bring to the job for which you are interviewing.

Take a look at the following critical traits and skills employers seek in candidates. Do they not apply equally to your personal endeavors as well as your work life?

Leadership	Managing others
Negotiations	Project planning
Communications	Problem-solving
Presentations	Report writing
Persuasiveness	Sacrifice
Team-building	Creative thinking
Team player	Practice to perfection
Dealing with conflict	Crisis management
Running meetings	Team involvement
Chairing committees	Delegation
Burning the "midnight oil"	Coaching
Short-handed	Risk-taking
Under tight time constraints	Motivation
Learning new things	Recognition

The list is endless and so are the opportunities to illustrate skills, traits, and accomplishments that cross over from work to personal, and visa versa. Take an inventory of all your personal accomplishments, what it required to achieve them, and the elements that are transferable to a work environment. Scour your past involvement in community activities, social organizations, professional societies, faith-based activities, volunteer work, scouts, children's school activities and parent groups, hobbies, sports, reading interests, music, and so on. Also, include university-related activities, tasks, organizations, and so on, in order to demonstrate your achievements while you were attending college.

Next, convert the information into useable responses to behavioral interviewing questions. Practice them so that you can express them intelligently, smoothly, and using high-impact phrases. Add these to your work-related achievements for which you have also scripted behavioral interviewing responses. Your goal is to be flexible, versatile, and creative in your responses to a particular behavioral question. Dazzle the interviewer with different situations and be prepared for when the person says, *"That is good, but tell me about another situation."* (Hint: Don't appear too rehearsed.) Give the question some thought and reach into your inventory and pull out an example that best fits the situation. Remember: The objective is to be in control of the interview or discussion, and to provide real-life circumstances that elevate your candidacy standing.

Chapter Worksheet

List here all of your personal accomplishments and activities. Begin with the most significant and continue to write everything that comes to your mind, even things that seem inconsequential or easily achieved, as they can be an example of things you do well (where others have difficulty).

	Activity	Accomplishments	Skills Involved
1.			
2.			
3.			
4.			
5.			
6.			
7.			
8.			
9.			
10.			

11.

12.

13.

14.

15.

16.

17.

18.

19.

20.

Now script the most remarkable accomplishments into behavioral-interviewing responses. What was the circumstance? What was expected of you? How did you go about tackling it? What were the results? What did it mean to you and others?

	Situation	Behavioral Response
1.		
2.		
3.		
4.		
5.		
6.		
7.		
8.		
9.		
10.		

CHAPTER 7

Reference Phrases

The job interview gets down to the stage where the company is planning on extending an offer, but first checking your references. It is the authors' experience that reference checks take on two forms: (1) a detailed, exhaustive check of your references, or (2) a routine, perfunctory audit of several or all of your references.

The very best way to ensure that you will get a stellar reference is to retain control of the process to the greatest extent possible. Make sure you know what is going to be said before it is ever said. That way, if a reference is not as good as you would like, eliminate that person from your list. The best way to do this it to get written references prior to the interview. It can eliminate the reference check altogether for a few reasons. Some hiring managers and human resources professionals will be satisfied that their reference check is done. Others will assume that they will get little additional benefit from calling, as they have the information in front of them.

Let's now discuss what happens if you are able to get written references beforehand, or if the firm require its standard reference check in addition to the letters you have submitted. As mentioned, there are exhaustive reference checks, as well as brief audits. Let's look closer at both types.

The first type of reference checking is extensive and information sensitive. It is very thorough and turns up significant information and insight. Some of the feedback may be contrary to what was learned in the interviews. That is okay as the goal is to weigh everything and make a sound decision based upon the facts. This scenario assumes that the decision to hire will not be final until references are completed and evaluated.

The second type of reference checking is based upon the fact that the decision to hire has already been made. Essentially the desire is to do a "spot" check of references. Except for incredulous or damaging information that would prohibit any firm from hiring the candidate, the company really wants to turn up information that supports its decision. Hence, short, positive reference responses satisfy this expectation. The longer the reference call goes, the greater the possibility that a "deficiency" or "shortcoming" might surface, and this would interrupt the process.

In both instances the candidate needs to be proactive with the company and with her or his designated references. As discussed throughout this book, the intent here is to not present yourself (or prep your references to present you) as something other than what you truly are. The objective is to frame the picture taken of you as an excellent fit. You need to steer the company towards the most valuable insights and accomplishments with a past employer, and you want to arm those who have volunteered to give a reference with the information that corroborates the same. Power phrases are critical here.

Unfortunately, the reference section on an employment application, if you are asked to complete one, is short on space. Never do you want to leave names and numbers of references without qualifying them. Take time to word process a list of references, when best to contact them, and their mail and e-mail addresses, as well as work, home, and cell, if possible, numbers. Provide a modicum of commentary—that is, how long the person has known you, the specifics of the work or personal relationship (titles, locations, company, and so on), and the areas of performance or work competencies about which the individual is well-suited to discuss. Here are some examples:

▸ "Ben was my immediate supervisor at Mobility Corporation from 1997 to 2003. As Production Manager, he was responsible for 12 first-line supervisors, including me, who directed the work of 230 hourly people. It was with Ben that I prepared and presented the findings of the lean manufacturing roll out. He also was a great aid in helping me address personnel issues the moment they occurred. As a result of my unit's production numbers, Ben promoted me to department manager."

▸ "Sally worked for me as a marketing analyst for three years in early 2000. She can vouch for my coaching skills and commitment to improve team-member performance. When Sally transferred into my department she was on a performance improvement plan. Although I could have gone through the motions with this plan and ultimately terminated her, I saw potential there and acknowledged that it would take some work on my part as well as hers. She responded well to my suggestions. She can talk to the way I supervise, communicate, and motivate my employees, as well as how I deal with performance problems."

▸ "Jessie is a sales representative with Acme Parts and has been calling on our company for 12 years. We have interacted as seller and buyer for the last two years. He has told me numerous times how much more organized I am than previous incumbents in the position. He always drives a hard sale and can comment upon my creative approaches to win-win negotiations on supplier terms."

▸ "Martina and I cochaired, during 2004 and 2005, the 'Campaign for Greatness' campaign to raise funds to buy and develop 28 acres of land bordering the town into a four- seasons sporting complex. She can attest to my ability to mobilize volunteers to create, conduct, and analyze a town-wide needs survey."

▸ "Laurence was the General Manager of the Midwest Sales and Service operation of ABC Company during my term of employment. Although I did not work directly for Larry, I was part of his zero-defects committee. I initially was skeptical of the concept and he was critical of that. He can attest to the personal effort I put in to understand the process and change my attitude and become one of the greatest proponents of program."

In each instance you have provided the person with exacting information regarding your work relationship and accomplishments. Will the company, when it calls these individuals, focus on this information? You may never know. Regardless, you have left a positive imprint regarding one more bit of information about you. Perhaps the message you convey is just one more "tell me about a time" scenario, one that did not surface during your interviews. Thus it has one more example of your ability to bring about results, and your reference, whether asked or not, can volunteer the details.

So you have covered the bases with the interviewing company, but how about your references? The best approach to soliciting help from business and personal references is to refresh their memory. Sure, they can capably handle a reference call with little or no notice. They, however, can do a much better job and will feel more secure if they know what they might be asked and how they can accurately respond to the questions or volunteer information that will enhance your candidacy. So how do you do that?

First, you call your references ahead of time to discuss your career initiative and the company with whom you are interviewing. Be straightforward about the job, the responsibilities, and the fit you see. Your references, if they truly know you, will be supportive of you once they know the job is within your capabilities. If they don't, they will tell you. Share with the reference what you communicated during your interviews about the two of you. Jog their memory, if necessary: "Remember the time we worked together on the Wilson account? How we pulled off the impossible?"

Next, follow up with an e-mail or letter and elaborate on what you initially talked about. Here is an example:

> Larry,
> Thank you for volunteering as a reference for me with the ABC job opportunity. As I mentioned during our telephone conversation, this company is big on the use of proven project-management techniques and disciplines. You remember a number of projects that I worked on, including:
> 1. The development of the auto-track system for querying customer-order status with manufacturing. It resulted in our ability to track, for the first time ever, work in progress and projected-delivery dates. It also increased our customer satisfaction ratings from 82 percent to 93 percent.

2. As part of your multifacility team, I worked on identifying eight key barriers in the production process that blocked on-time completion. Using the delta process re-engineering tools I was able to recommend low-cost, high-results solutions.

3. Lastly, we worked together on a high-profile project assigned by Mark Killingsly, the President. He wanted us to come up with a 30-percent cycle time improvement on welding processes. You remember exactly what we did there as we received the "2003 Make a Difference Award."

You know I would be an excellent fit for this new position. It is a logical step for me, having just completed my M.B.A. It will be a challenge for me, but you know I am always up for such. Working hard and smart has always been a motto for me.

Thanks again for the support. I have always valued our friendship and working past.

Now you have everything covered. During your interview you relayed numerous examples of your accomplishments at your former place of employment. They may or may not ask your reference(s) about the events. Your reference(s) in turn has (have) been reminded of other achievements and the metrics that go along with the effort. The net result is a wide path of achievement, all real, and all of importance.

You will often find that after a former employer or other relevant individual provides you with a written reference, assuming it was a good reference, he or she will feel even more positive about you. This is for several psychological reasons. One major contributor is cognitive dissonance. Cognitive dissonance is a theory of human motivation that asserts that it is psychologically uncomfortable to hold contradictory thoughts. For example, if I said good things about you, I must feel that they must be true (even if they weren't). It would be psychologically uncomfortable for me to say good things about you and believe them not to be true. So if I say it, I end up believing it. You can see where all the advantages are in this.

A tip, however, for you: Never script what you want your reference(s) to say when called. It will sound staged. Simply provide your reference(s) with overviews of various situations and let them use their own words. Then it is them and it is real. Your calls help set the tone, and your e-mail or letter will help with the call from the company.

In the worksheet that follows, identify your main and backup references. Who are they? How do they know you? When was that? What is it that they know about you and can speak about in detail? Do they need reminders about some of your achievements? What do you want to relay to them in your call for help, and in your follow-up letter of facts and figures?

Verifying Educational Degrees

Many employers make it a practice to verify the degrees stated in your resume and on the application form. Never falsely state your education degrees. Although you may feel it is necessary to "stretch" the truth, understand that it is wrong, and in some circumstances illegal, to misstate your degrees. Today most institutions of higher learning have online verification tools or share their records and databases with reference verification organizations. Now, in a matter of minutes, a company can (and will) confirm your degree(s).

Some people keep on file photocopies of their degrees or transcripts. Some companies will not accept these as confirmation of a degree. For confirmation letters or transcripts from the school, companies may require the presence of a raised seal of the institution.

Chapter Worksheet

Reference #1:

Reference #2:

Reference #3:

Reference #4:

Reference #5:

Additionally, you will find it to be helpful to understand what kind of questions are usually asked in a reference check so you will know what to discuss with your references before the fact. Here are examples of a standard set of questions used by many individuals who check references:

Applicant Name:

Applied for Position:

Recruiter:

Date of Reference:

Reference Provider:

Position:

Company/Phone:

In what capacity did/do you know the candidate (title)?

How long have you known him/her (dates of employment)?

What was/is his/her reason for leaving?

How was his/her attendance and punctuality? Please explain.

What were the candidate's primary responsibilities?

How would you describe the candidate's knowledge of his/her job? How would you assess his/her on the job performance?

Can you give me an example of how the candidate performed above the expectations of his/her current job? (Was he/she able to think out of the box? If so, how?)

Could you give me an example of how he/she took responsibility for his/her actions on the job?

What were the candidate's strengths? What does he/she do particularly well?

What weaknesses or other issues did you observe that detracted from the quality of work?

What are two areas you would like to see him/her develop?

Please comment on the candidate's work ethic and integrity. Did you ever have cause to question it?

Is the candidate eligible for rehire? Would you rehire him/her? Why/why not?

The candidate is under consideration for a position requiring (give the position's name) and doing (give a brief description of skills/duties). Please describe how you think she/he will do in this job. Why?

Please make any additional comments. What else should we, as a potential employer, know about this candidate?

Note: Ask additional questions that address specific managers' concerns!!!

CHAPTER 8

Understanding Behavioral and Communicative Styles

The well-known character, Dr. Doolittle, had a famous song, "Talk to the Animals." What an advancement that would be, to understand how to communicate directly with creatures of the earth. The same really applies to humans! If only we knew how to communicate with others in the way they like to be communicated with.

Well, the folks at Targeted Training International have developed a way to identify the different communication styles of individuals. The tool is called DISC, and it has been around for decades. Each of us has a dominant behavioral style that determines how we receive communications. There are four different styles. All are present (in varying levels) in everyone, but one tends to stand out above the others. That is often called the *core style*. These four styles are: Dominance, Influence, Steadiness, and Compliance. Here are overviews of each style.

Dominance: How one responds to problems and challenges. A person who is a high *D* is very direct in his or her actions.

Ds are task-, not people-, oriented. This means that they are focused on getting the job done, immediately, and with little concern for people and relationships. Ds have a need to control. In DISC language a D is known as a *driver*.

Influence: How one influences others to his or her point of view. A high I, as does the D, moves rapidly but is more concerned with being involved with people. An I has little regard for routines and can be very impulsive. His or her orientation is toward people, not tasks. Is are focused on the future and what is exciting to them. If only one word were allowed when describing a high **I** it would be "expressive."

Steadiness: How one responds to the pace of the environment. A high S's focus is on today in terms of time frame and on relating with others. The S seeks predictability and avoids conflict(s). Similar to an I, an S is people-, not task-, oriented. An S can support change only after he or she thoroughly understands the implications and if he or she is not rushed. An S is often described as "amiable."

Compliance: How one respond to rules and procedures. A high C works in a historical time frame and his or her focus is on gathering information in order to make decisions or recommendations. A C has a need to organize. A C is task-, not people-, oriented, and reacts very slowly and cautiously (because of the need for information). The DISC terminology for a C is "analytical."

There are guidelines for communicating to people of each core style. If you adhere to these talking points you will be much more effective in reaching the other party during conversations. If you don't match the communication style then you are less likely to be understood, and you may even lose or alienate the other person. Obviously, as is Dr. Doolittle's, your goal is to talk his or her talk!

In learning about the four styles, there are three things you will need to know. First, what are the driving behaviors of each style and how each prefers to communicate and receive communications. You need to know what the person is all about, and what his or her focus is.

Second, you need to know how you can go about spotting the style in someone else. Otherwise you will not know how to blend your communications to his or her style. You can deduce a lot about a person and his or her style by observing his or her actions and surroundings. How does he or she talk? What does he or she talk about, and what hand motions accompany his or her words? If you are interviewing in his or her office, what does it look like? How is he or she organized? Where are both of you sitting during the interview? For how long is the interview scheduled, and how long does it actually last?

Third, what phrases and phrasings are most effective with each style? How do you approach your answers? What should you say? What words and phrases are most effective? What gets one's attention?

Let's spend some time learning about each style, the likes and dislikes of each in terms of communications, how to spot the style, and what phrases to use:

High *D* (Drivers)

Remember, a *D*'s entire focus is responding to problems and challenges. The *D* is concerned about getting things done and is results-oriented. The type is best known as a "driver." The focus is on tasks, not people. They are very direct in their conversation—no small talk, and to the point. When talking or interviewing with a *D* you also need to be direct and to the point. Don't ramble. Don't small talk or waste time. Don't get personal with the individual unless asked. Be organized and logical in your communication. Stick to facts and figures and be prepared to back up what you say. A *D* does not like slow or rambling talkers. Be brisk in your talking and exude confidence. If you see signs of impatience, such as finger-tapping or restlessness, then you are talking too much or too long.

Remember that a high *D* is all about results and achievements, so express and talk about yourself in a similar manner. A *D* almost always will control the interview. He or she will have an objective when talking with you. CEOs, executives, and senior management personnel are often *D* types, as they are achievers and the positions call for task focused results.

Although a small percentage of the overall population (14 percent), a *D* is easy to identify. He or she is very direct in conversations, and quick in actions. Although extroverted, a *D* is not overly friendly. So, when you see the conversation dealing primarily with tasks, activities, and accomplishments instead of people, relationships, and personal things, you are dealing with a *D*. You will notice that a *D*'s office is sparse. The desk will be totally or somewhat clean, the in-basket empty, and few accessories around the room. Where there are pictures, they will be achievement-oriented (accomplishments recorded through pictures—that is, mountain climbing, bicycling, golf tournament score card, and so on.). Pictures of family or one's spouse will be limited to one or two. You will find yourself across the desk from a *D* or on the other side of a coffee table. The *D*'s posture will be firm and rarely relaxed. His or her hand motions while talking will be sharp, accentuated, and with purpose. The hands will stay relatively close to the body. All these signals point toward a business-orientation. The *D* will take and retain control of the interview from the very beginning. Indeed, aside from a perfunctory inquiry of "how are you?", or "how are things going today?" the *D* will not show personal interest. The *D* is interested in who you are professionally, what you have accomplished, and what you will do for him or her and for the company.

The high *D* reacts favorably to action words and phrases that reflect results. The bottom line is more important than the details leading up to, or involved in, accomplishing it. Brevity is important. The *D* will ask for more information if it is important. Be factual, but not detailed. When you do not know the answer to a question, say so instead of trying to talk around or out of it. The *D* is interested in the "what" you have done, so you make sure you tell her or him exactly that. Do it with brevity and with facts and numbers. He or she may ask you how you achieved the results. Again, be factual and brief.

Tell me about yourself.

▸ "I am a results-oriented marketing manager who sets high standards and goals. For example, I created new marketing brochures and one-sheets highlighting the effectiveness and applications of our products. These were done in three weeks, and at half the cost of prior initiatives." [Note the brevity of the statement and inclusion of facts and results.]

▸ "For the past 5 years I consistently exceeded difficult sales quotas by 25 to 38 percent through segmentation of my customers and sales potential. My margins were in the top 10th percentile of the sales force and this resulted in my receiving the President's Club award four out of the 5 years."

▸ "I have always set high goals for myself at work and away from work. I like the challenge of learning new things and applying the principles learned. For example, I am a firm believer in process improvement techniques. Using Six-Sigma methodology I brought down production cycle times by 35 percent."

▸ "I set a goal several years ago of kayaking, solo, a 60-mile stretch of Colorado River involving rapids and portage around major waterfalls. I did it in four days, which put me in the top quartile of all who have accomplished this feat." [Note: always link personal interests to some form of metric or accomplishment.]

▶ "I am a five-handicap golfer." [As opposed to "I enjoy playing golf."]

Tell me about your college days.

▶ "I set and accomplished many goals during my four years." [Give examples and achievements.]

▶ "Without sacrificing my grades I played forward on the varsity basketball team all four years. We were Division III NCAA quarterfinalists two of those years and national champions in my senior year." [Put forth examples of challenges and accomplishments.]

▶ "Because I took some college-level classes in high school and my advanced placement test scores in some subjects gave me immediate credits, I was able to complete my degree in 3½ years." [Action and results]

What do you know about our company?

▶ "My research shows that the company has performed exceptionally well the last three years with gross sales of [cite numbers]."

▶ "That it seeks individuals who can work in a fast-paced environment and assess situations and make decisions with limited information." [pace, action, control]

What can you do for me? [This is a favorite question of a *D*.]

▶ "One of my strengths is the ability to take limited information and make intelligent assessments of the market. You can rely on me to make intelligent decisions in a timely manner." [decision-maker, fast-paced]

▶ "I can help you improve your business unit result in the order of [cite percentage or number result] by [cite how you would do it]."

What questions do you have of me?

▶ "Which is more important to the future of the company, growing market share or margin [Ds like to be in control by deciding] and why [Ds like to give opinions]?"

Why are you looking? Why do you want to leave?

▶ "The environment is very consensus-oriented and decisions are not made in a timely, efficient fashion. I have to wait for a green light on most all of my work. I am capable and willing to make decisions in shorter time frames and with less information. I am not afraid of being held accountable." [Remember that a high *D* is results-oriented and can relate to this type of statement. He or she might even ask you what could be done to improve the situation.]

Although the *D* may put forth social courtesies, keep in mind that this person is really about business and nothing else. He or she is a results oriented, fast-decision-making type. Your questions of the interviewer and your answers to his or her questions should be quick, concise, and decisive. Skip the small talk and get right to it.

High *I* (Expressives)

As highlighted earlier, an *I* is all about dealing with people and making contacts. A high *I* likes to interact and relate. He or she is a very expressive type, and his or her efforts revolve around people and contacts. When communicating with a high *I* be prepared to chat and socialize. Relating is important to the interviewer, so take time to ask about him or her and to let him or her get to know you. He or she will let you know when it is time to interview, so don't shift gears without him or her being ready. An *I* is very extroverted and, to a fault, very impulsive. As opposed to the high *D,* a high *I* is action-oriented for the fun of it (versus for the results with a *D*). Extremely optimistic, a high *I* has a "can do" attitude despite the facts of the situation. He or she is not detail-oriented and not a strong planner. Positions such as the heads of human resources, marketing, public relations, communications, executive assistants, and so on, may be predominately *I* types.

You will recognize a high *I* by his or her unbridled enthusiasm. An *I* (28 percent of the general population) is gregarious and most likely will dominate the interview. Because he or she is not concerned about routines or procedures, the interview may jump around from topic to topic, as if there is no order. Interviews with an *I* most likely will begin with getting to know one another. This socializing is important to an *I*. The time frame for an *I* is now and tomorrow, the future, and he or she will ask about your dreams and goals for work and for you, personally. Family may be mentioned, but the real focus is you and the high *I*. You will find a high *I* to be somewhat (or even highly) disorganized. His or her desk and office will have piles of papers, reports, and binders. There may be some family pictures on the credenza or wall, but these will be overwhelmed by relationship pictures of the high *I* with others: events with community people, colleagues, company outings, sales meetings, the golf foursome, and so on. The high *I* will speak rapidly, and be very animated with his or her voice inflections and hand movements. The hands will mostly likely be always moving, and in broad, extended physical gestures. Your interview will most likely take place in an informal setting with no spatial barriers between you.

When interviewing with a high *I* you have to remember to exercise some control with the meeting, as the *I* may wander and forget to ask important questions about you and the position. When you are relaying your achievements and work responsibilities always inject excitement about what you do or have accomplished. Include testimonials from prior bosses, customers, or clients (whether external or internal). Do not overload the *I* with facts and data, but rather focus on reiterating and reinforcing one or two key things about you. Unless the *I* is taking voluminous notes, which rarely happens with this behavioral style, he or she will not remember all that was said and the points you made. Hence, you want to firmly plant the big picture of you. A high *I* can be misleading. You may walk away from the interview believing that you are a "shoe-in" based upon the *I*'s enthusiasm. Remember to ask for his or her opinion about the company, the job, the work involved, and your background in order to clarify the interviewer's very positive demeanor.

Tell me about yourself.

▸ "I am an accomplished production manager who enjoys leading others in producing a quality product of which customers can be proud. My unit director regards me as a valued member of the leadership team and has said that my enthusiasm spills over to all in the department. I enjoy getting results through people." [Note the spirit of the statement, the mention of someone important, and the testimonial.]

▸ "My entire career has been devoted to being future-oriented; anticipating the skills and know-how I must have in order to be successful at work and developing a plan to achieve them."

▸ "People say that I am creative in my job and adept at influencing others to my ideas."

▸ "My colleagues regard me as a strong team player who can be counted on when deadlines draw near or when someone is absent."

▸ "I have been thinking for sometime about making a major career move, one to an organization that can fully tap my writing and editing skills. I have many ideas that are not being embraced by my current employer. Is your company one that encourages and makes use of employee creativity?" [Note the asking of one's opinion.]

▸ "There is so much to me. Where would you like me to begin?"

What do you know about our company?

▸ "I know several people who work here and they relay that this is a place where people work hard but have fun doing it. I like to be part of an organization that involves its people, asks their opinions, and promotes teamwork." [A high I is always in the moment and the excitement of the work, and likes testimonials.]

▸ I have known of XYZ for a number of years and view them as a respectable place to work and an organization that values the contributions of its employees. But tell me what you like about it and why you joined them. [You can substitute many statements for the first sentence. It is the second sentence, asking the interviewer why he or she likes the company, which is important here. A high I likes to talk and expound on who he or she is and why the company is great. The I likes to hear himself or herself talk; give them that opportunity!]

Tell me about your dreams and aspirations. [a favorite question of an I]

▸ "I enjoy the challenge of working with others and making things fun while accomplishing our work."

▸ "I have a long-term goal of becoming a vice president of public relations. It is something which I would enjoy and be good at." [Note: If you said this to a high D, you should be prepared to quickly state how you will achieve this goal.

With the *I*, however, you want to talk about why
you like the profession.]

What questions do you have of me?

You definitely want to ask questions, as there most likely
are things you want answers to or want to know more about.
Regardless of the questions, make sure that you open the question with, "What do you think about....," or, "What is your
opinion on....," or, "What would you suggest I do....," as a
high *I* enjoys giving opinions. Also you should ask questions
dealing with the future and the people you would be working
with or for, as an *I* is a here-and-on thinker and is relationship
focused.

> ▸ "How would you describe the people here at
> [name company]?" [The response will immedi-
> ately tell you if he or she is an *I*.]

Why are you looking? Why do you want to leave?

> ▸ "The work environment is very cold and cut-
> throat. People are not valued for their contribu-
> tions and ideas, nor are they encouraged to work
> as a team." [Again, an *I* is about people, relating,
> making work enjoyable, and so on, so frame your
> answers in such terms. As with all your answers,
> however, it must always be truthful, yet phrased
> to appeal to the person's style.]

Always remember that the high *I* is someone who is *in the
moment* and very expressive. Be optimistic with him or her,
talk about dreams and aspirations, seek his or her opinions
(avoid expressing counter opinions of your own), complement
him or her, and, in general, be open to an interview that may
wander in content and change quickly. [If you are a high *S* or
C this person will be your boss. Ask yourself if you can work
for someone such as this, or how you can manage communications so you can do your job.]

High *S* (Amiables)

Remember that a high *S* is about steadiness and how one responds to the pace of the environment. An *S* is about consistency, predictability, reliability, and so on. An *S*'s behavior is primarily introverted and, as a result, he or she is usually quiet and reserved. His or her orientation, similar to that of the high *I*, is towards people. A high *S* is about relating and developing trust (that is, amiable in behavior). Trust must be present before moving forward for a *S*. This style is conflict-adverse but, if necessary, will deal with conflict. Because change represents newness and possible conflict, an *S* is slow to buy into change. You will find an *S* in positions such as human resources, customer service, accounting, and other jobs where steadiness is important, as an *S* likes to think, review, and wait through things.

This is a very common style (40 percent of the general population) and understandably so. This class of people provides stability to our work and personal lives, and that is how you can identify an *S*—by the pace of his or her talk and actions. A high *S*, in an interview, will be personal and try to make you feel comfortable. You will see a genuine interest in who you are and why you are pursuing the position. The high *S* is normally soft-spoken, reflective, and informal (although not always relaxed) in the interview. You may have to exercise patience as with the *S* when listening to him or her. You will immediately see warmth and friendliness in his or her office or work station. There will be many pictures of family and relatives; the desk and work area will be somewhat neat and orderly. The pace of talk and use of hand gestures will be drawn out. They will not talk in a rushed manner, nor does the high *S* like to be rushed. Body language and hand movements will be subtle and slower paced than a high *D* or *I*. His or her hands will move within a limited radius of the body. If you talk about something new, or something that involves change, you will see a look of hesitation on an *S*'s face. The look will fade once he or she feels more assured or comfortable with the idea.

When interviewing with *S*s you must help them feel relaxed and work towards developing trust. Ironically, they too will be working to the same goal. This is difficult when it is the first time you have met, but during the course of the interview, if you take time to elaborate about yourself (and in a soft voice), you will begin to relate. The *S* wants to control the pace of the interview and is a question-asking individual. Follow his or her direction, do not wander in your answers, and respond with questions such as, "Was that helpful?" Families are important to an *S* so, where appropriate, bring yours into the conversation. Do not rush to the next topic or issue, but wait for them to change gears.

Tell me about yourself.

▸ "I am married with two teenage children. My wife is an accountant and I am a software developer who enjoys working on project teams chartered with designing new business systems." [Note the inclusion of family.]

▸ "My area of expertise and experience is in process-improvement systems. I find that I am most productive in environments where teamwork is encouraged and, although I am not intimidated by tight deadlines, I work best when there is sufficient time to complete projects in a quality manner and thoroughly audit all documentation." [Note the reference to steady pace.]

▸ "As you can see from my resume, I am not one to jump quickly from one employer to the next. I view this as being disloyal. Instead, I prefer to be making long-term contributions to the organization, all the while personally growing. With my current employer I completed my master's degree. I had hoped that it would result in advancement in my department but it hasn't. That is one of the reasons I believe it is time to make a career change."

What do you know about our company?

▶ "I have watched your company steadily grow over the years and believe this to be a result of not rushing into things, but rather taking the time to develop market-sensitive products."

▶ "You have a history of planned, organized change. I like that kind of environment—you know, where things are well thought-out."

Tell me about your dreams and aspirations.

▶ "My long-term goals for work are realistic and result from many hours of contemplation and review of my talents and interests. If I am patient and work hard I believe I can be a [title or function] by/within [state age or number of years]." [An *S* wants to know that you have not rushed into this decision, and that it is logical and orderly.]

What questions do you have of me?

▶ "Talk to me about the way people work together and relate with one another."

▶ "How would you describe the sociability of this company?"

▶ "Although I have been in many situations where decisions have to be made quickly, my best work results when I take the time to double check it and share it with colleagues before it is final. How are decisions made here?" [If the individual is truly an *S* your approach is very compatible and desired.]

Why are you looking? Why do you want to leave?

▶ "The company is very cold and impersonal. Information is not shared and decisions rushed.

Employees are neither trusted nor respected." [Remember that an *S* is about relationships and pace.]

In summary, always keep a steady pace with your questions and answers. Don't rush or exaggerate. Be warm and work on building trust. With out using the words "trust" or "respect" give examples of your work and relationships where this is true. The *S* is weary of change when it is occurs without explanation, discussion, or personal involvement. Explain how you have made improvements and changes by doing the latter route.

High *C* (Analyticals)

People with strong *C* tendencies are very rule- and procedure-oriented. They are most comfortable when guidelines exist, and significant information is available. They are all about procedures and compliance. They are very task-oriented and introverted in work behavior. The milieu of a high *C* is historical because that is where the data trail lies. The *C* is very chronologically oriented and applies logic to everything he or she does. The *C* normally must have lots of information before moving forward or making a decision; otherwise uneasiness sets in. High *C*s make excellent engineers, quality-assurance people, accounting or numbers-related positions, or administrators. A high *C* is occasionally found in a leadership role if the company is of a scientific or technical nature, but in general a *C* is not effective in a CEO's role because he or she cannot make speedy decisions. A *C* needs lots of information before deciding and can get locked into an "analysis-paralysis" mode.

The *C* category is the least populated (14 percent of all people), but is a very necessary group in terms of credibility, benchmarking, and verifying information. Despite their small numbers, they are easy to spot. First of all, they are well-organized, as you would expect. You will find a *C*'s office to not always be neat, but definitely organized in terms of files, bookshelves, paper piles, computer reports, charts, and graphs. Family pictures will be very limited in number and the walls and work areas will have framed certificates, degrees, patent awards, and so on. Reference manuals, scientific reports, FAQs, and so on, will also be on hand. The *C* will be very nonemotional when engaged in a conversation or interview, and guarded with his or her body language. You will see little or no hand movement while he or she is talking, and what does occur will be kept very close to the body. Being task-oriented, the high *C* will ask many questions in order to gather as much information as needed in order to render a decision or opinion.

When interviewing with a *C* make sure you offer up plenty of facts, situations, and information. Be much more detailed than when talking with a *D*, an *I*, or even an *S*. Present in a logical, organized fashion so that one thing leads to the next. Do not hesitate to ask questions such as, "Does that help you?", "Do you want me to cover more?", or "Is there anything else you want to know or ask?" If there is silence on the interviewer's behalf, do not talk, as he or she is thinking! Also, do not hesitate to ask questions of your own, as it is style compatible, and it will result in very useful information for you.

Tell me about yourself.

▸ "Well, I graduated from college in 1987 with a major in psychology and a GPA of 3.7. In June of the same year I began work with ACF Company, where I still work. My first job was as a job analyst where I gathered information on the job and tasks, wrote descriptions, and evaluated their relative worth [be prepared to explain how you did such]. Two years later I was promoted to a human resource specialist, where I learned to conduct job interviews and place candidates in jobs.

My initial analyst position helped me greatly as an interviewer as I understood the job content. Recently I was offered a position in another state but I declined after doing a detailed analysis of the cost of living and school systems for my children." [chronological, detailed, and illustrative of thought processes]

What would you like to know? [A fair question, as it helps you zero in on what is important to the interviewer.]

▸ "I recently completed my master's degree in operations management. It required attending classes every Friday evening and all day Saturday for two years. My thesis was on utility theory and dealt with perceived versus real outputs resulting from having limited historical production data."

▸ "My entire career has been devoted to being future-oriented anticipating the skills and know-how I must have in order to be successful at work and developing a plan to achieve them."

What do you know about our company?

▸ "I have known of your company for more than [state number] years. Your size [state size of company in sales or number of employees] is just right and your annual growth rate [state] is impressive. Your goal is to state facts and figures as the *C* is a detail person."

Tell me about your dreams and aspirations.

▸ "For [x] years I have been working on a plan to become a [state objective] by the time I am [state age]. It requires that I do the following: [give details]." [The *C* is all about minutiae, measurements, magnitudes, and extensive planning.]

What questions do you have of me?

▸ "What are the details going into the [cite a plan, decision, work approach, and so on]?" [Take your time; I am very interested how you quantify things here. Give the interviewer permission to go into depth with his or her answer. After all, that is the style of a *C*.]

Why are you looking? Why do you want to leave?

▸ "For the past [state the months or years] I have been assessing my future and value with the company. My work involves [go into detail] but I am capable of doing more, such as [cite]." [A *C* wants to hear exactness.]

In general your own questions and answers to the interviewer's questions should be thoughtful and exacting. Don't hesitate to go into extra detail. Be prepared for follow-up questions/statements of a qualifying or quantifying nature, such as "Exactly how did you do that?", or "Tell me more."

Summary

Zeroing in on the style of the interviewer, or potential boss, is very helpful in terms of how you communicate and frame your responses to questions, and knowing what questions to ask during the interview. Sometimes you can secure information in advance about the person you are to meet. Perhaps someone in your network knows the individual. If you are being sent in for an interview by a recruitment firm, the person who initially contacted you should know a few things about the hiring manager. Do not hesitate to ask the human resources representative who is facilitating your visit to describe the people you will be interviewing. Just as information about the company, its history, mission, and products, services, markets, and the job position is vital, so is information about the interviewers.

There will be more than one occasion in which you will meet or talk with the hiring manager and the human resources representative. Your first meeting will tell you much about his or her style. Use this information when you send your thank-you letters or e-mails and when you are in telephone communication. Knowing the interviewer's style (*D, I, S,* or *C*) will point you in the proper direction with respect to your phrasing of future communications. For example when corresponding after the interview:

Corresponding to a D

Be direct and to the point. Summarize the skills you bring to the job, your strengths, and the added value or outcomes that will result from joining the company. Highlight, in brief, bullet form, no more than four key attributes of you and the job.

Writing to an I

Relay how much you enjoyed meeting with the person and how your regard the person as your future boss. Express how you look forward to contributing to an exciting environment and making a difference in the job.

Penning a Note to an S

Express appreciation for the time spent with him or her and the opportunity to get to know one another. State how comfortable you would feel working for the individual and that your skills would blend in very well. Let the person know you can be trusted.

Following up With a C

Thank the individual for spending quality time going over the details of the job and learning about you. Place, in lengthy bullet form, five or six of the key traits about you, and how they match the candidate specifications or needs of the hiring manager.

Understanding the four basic styles also provides insight into your own makeup. Perhaps you have taken a DISC assessment instrument and you know your core style(s).

Use this information to your benefit when interviewing in person or on the telephone. Recognize situations where your style could be in conflict with that of the other person. Learn to shift or adapt your style to what you believe to be the style of the other person. For example, if you are a very detailed person (*C* style) and have a tendency to talk at length about facts and information but are dealing with a *D*-style person (problem-solver) then you need to work at being brief and to the point. In the same fashion, if you are an *I* style and in a conversation with a *C* person, you must force yourself to tone down your speaking and add details to what you are talking about.

Here is some general advice for you during an interview if you know your own style (and regardless of whether you know the style of the interviewer). The best thing to do is to center yourself, stylewise, so that your conversations, behavior, and phrasing of questions and answers are within the other's "comfort zone." This means:

If Your Style Is Most Similar to the D's

Work at decelerating your pace of speech. Avoid short, punchy responses and straight yes or no answers. Exhibit a bit more warmth and be more engaging, be more conversational (particularly with small talk), and don't jump into your answers. Remember that your style is less than 20 percent of the general population and unless you are across from another *D* you should be less directive and controlling.

Should I Be Your Core Style

A high *I* usually knows he or she is that style! You must concentrate on the topical nature of the questions and your answers. Don't ramble on and on or wander. Be more succinct in your speech. Be conscious of your pace of speech and do not, repeat, do not go forever with your answers or go off topic. Exhibit some restraint with your voice level and arm movements.

If You See That You Are an S Style

As an amiable type there is little you need to do (40 percent of the population belong to this category). You should, however, slightly increase the pace of your speech, and exert more modulation in your voice, too. Gesture with your hands, as you always do. The most important thing is to be open to surprises, new information or aspects of the job you were not anticipating. As an *S* (and *C* too) you need time to adapt to change and new situations. Subconsciously your facial movements may indicate apprehension, or even fear. Force yourself to keep those feeling internal, while externally reacting in a positive manner.

If You Recognize Yourself as a C Type

As an analytical person, unless you are across the interview desk from someone of the same style, you have to go easy on your quest for details. Don't go overboard on questions and clarifications. Learn to be comfortable, even though you are lacking all the information. Use more hand movements and facial gestures than you normally do.

One more thing about behavioral styles. Make note of the job description for the position you are pursuing. Most companies make the full description available during the interview process. Job descriptions usually contain a lengthy statement of the work responsibilities and the candidate specifications or requirements. If a job description is not available then go back and look at the wording of the recruitment advertisement. With a keen eye you will recognize a *D, I, S,* or *C* style within the description. Is the job one of problem-solving, leadership, and quick decision-making (*D*), or does it require outgoing, strong people skills (*I*)? Does it seek teamwork and collaborative skills (*S*), or deep analytical skills and a quality orientation (*C*)? The candidate specifications will be very revealing as to the type (style) of person needed.

These will be the style traits for which the interview team will be looking, despite their own style(s). Obviously, though you shouldn't mimic the expected style (unless it is the same as yours), you should adapt your communications and behavior in the interview to align closer with that required by the job. If you discover that you are uncomfortable with the style needed then this job may not be for you. Although you may think you are capable of accomplishing the job responsibilities and demands of the job, you will not be happy because of the style conflict, either with the job or with your boss.

Chapter Worksheet

- ▸ Do you have a sense of your core style? What are the attributes of this style?

- ▸ What do you know about the individual(s) you will be interviewing with?

- ▸ Any clue to his or her style?

- ▸ How can you learn more about the individual before going into the interview?

- ▸ Based upon your interactions and observations during the interview, what style do you believe best fits the individual(s) you are interviewing (or have interviewed) with and how might you use that to your advantage in future conversations or communications? What might you have to do to adapt your style in order to maximize connectivity?

- ▸ What do the job description and candidate specifications tell you about the ideal style for success and job satisfaction?

CHAPTER 9

Phrases That
Bridge Generations

Just as there are DISC-style differences between people, there are also generation gaps that exist between people. Never in the history of the United States has the workforce been comprised of four distinctly different generations of people. Each is a unique product of its years of youth and work experiences, imprinted by its families, social surroundings, the economy, and the politics of the time. Each generation relates best within, rather than between. Conflict, confusion, miscommunication, and contempt may surface between the generations and it is understandable when you fully grasp the unique traits of each.

To which generation do you belong? What about the individual(s) with whom you are communicating and interviewing? Do you understand the key differences in attitudes and behaviors between your generation and his or hers? You need to, because it is important to make use of this information when preparing for an interview, and when asking and answering questions during the interview.

The generations are determined by year of birth (plus or minus a couple of years). Each has its own "label," and having some insight into the people of each generation will aid you in interviewing and finding a job and environment that fits. The four generations and their basic tenets or traits are considered in the following paragraphs.

Traditionalists ("Matures")— Born Before 1945

It is all about experience! This is the group that went through World War II, the Korean Conflict, and the Cold War. Some personally went through the Depression of the 1930s, or they heard about it from their parents. These imprints taught them to live cautiously and conservatively, as well as to make sacrifices. Experience, to them, is the best teacher.

- ▸ Committed. Loyal to one another and to his or her employer (as the employer was to him or her). Tendency is to stay with same company for life. Takes/took care of his or her aged parents.

- ▸ Conformists. Looked for structure. Organizational charts in companies had many tiers and levels. SOPs (Standard Operating Procedures) are important.

- ▸ Respecting of institutions, including his or her church or temple.

- ▸ Most are now retired or have returned, out of financial necessity or boredom, to the workforce in a part-time capacity. These part-timers are filling the labor pool void in food service and retail businesses.

- ▸ Technologically challenged. Have (had) trouble adapting to computers, remote controls, and so on.

Baby Boomers—
Born Between 1946 and 1964

Question and challenge the past way of doing things. Reject the "status quo" and the institutions revered by the traditional generation.

▶ Believe that hard work and long hours are the way to get ahead. This workaholic attitude surfaced because of the stiff competition in the number of people in this group. Loyal, to a fault, to their employers. Work hard because they want to get ahead.

▶ Very success-oriented and use their financial gains to acquire (and show) things—cars, big houses, vacation homes, luxurious travel, expensive "toys," and so on. These indulgences sometimes carry over into the workplace in the form of abusing one's position.

▶ Fought for employee rights, nondiscrimination, equal opportunity, equality, and changes in the workplace.

▶ Optimistic. The "can do" generation. Creative. Responsible for the technological advances in the world.

Generation Xers (Gen Xers)—
Born Between 1965 and 1980

▶ Independent, resourceful, creative, and self-entertained. (They had to be because they are products of families where both parents work—these were the "latch-key kids," and the experience made them so.)

▸ Technology-adept. Grew up with the first video games, computers, and electronic toys. Very lasting imprint on this generation.

▸ Reject all that has come before because of what they have seen with their parents (divorce, loss of jobs, religion, politics, and so on).

▸ Committed to profession and work, but not to employer. Want work/life balance. Overtime not in the cards for them. Will often change jobs and employers (in part a product of portable 401(k) savings plans!) in order to advance.

▸ Unlike the optimistic Baby Boomers, can be pessimistic, critical, and cynical. Also have shorter time horizons. Want to get it done now.

▸ Less like a child in the family and more like a friend. Parents involved them in decisions.

The Millennials—Born Between 1980 and 2000

Growing up during Y2K! Not exactly adults compared with other generations. Most are still in school while some are just graduating from college and entering the workforce.

▸ Similar to the Gen Xers, their parents are also their friends. Their parents have also doted them, maybe even spoiled them.

▸ Very ambitious and optimistic but, in many ways, not certain what they really want to do.

▸ Technologically savvy. Grew up, literally from day one, with cell phones, PCs, PDAs, pagers, remote controls, DVDs, MP3s, and iPods. Adept at multitasking with these. Will do homework with TV on, with music coming from Walkman or MP3, or while on the computer instant messaging with friends. Not afraid of technology.

▸ Real or contrived, this group feels stressed and very busy.

Armed with information such as this will help you with inter- and intra-generational interviews. What should you be talking about with someone from the Baby Boomer era? With the GenX crowd? What about the generation that is fast disappearing from the workforce, the Matures? Or the newest members of the work population, the Milleniums?

Well, just as with DISC behavioral styles you must be aware of and sensitive to the differences between yourself and the other generation. If you are in the same grouping then you know intuitively what the person is about because you are one, too! Second, although some of the differences may frustrate you, zero in on the positives of that generation and talk to those during your interview. Lastly, find elements of compatibility or agreement that you can build upon in your discussion. In other words, although your generational roots and styles may be different, you obviously have certain skills, knowledge, business goals, and so on, that are common to both of you (For example, one of you is a Millenium and the other a Traditionalist, but you both have knowledge and appreciation of statistical models in predicting market success.)

---

1. Be aware of the person's roots.
2. Focus on the pluses.
3. Identify with tangibles, not subjective differences.

Communicating With Baby Boomers

Let's begin with the Baby Boomers, a group that will most likely be managing and running the company with whom you are interviewing. This generation is very competitive and has made sacrifices to get to where they are today. They want to be recognized for this and by the people they interview. Accustomed to working long hours and having a "whatever it takes" attitude, they expect you to do the same or suggest trade offs that still achieve the goal.

Although Baby Boomers are most likely proficient with computers, they did not grow up with such. Hence they most likely prefer personalized forms of communications: mail, notes, telephone calls, and so on. If you must use e-mail put some warmth into it, to the extent that you can. Never abbreviate your words in an e-mail. Baby Boomers are products of an educational system delivered by the Traditionalist! This means showing respect, honoring structure, and extending social courtesies. While you personally may reject their notion of work behaviors and practices, you must not openly say so (and alienate your chances for the job). Where you disagree with a principle—for example, working overtime—offer trade-offs or ideas for improved productivity (so you don't have to work long hours, and so on). Remember that this generation is the one that came up with the idea of "comp time," the practice of doing whatever it takes and receiving time off at a later time. This is a group that worked long hours at jobs that were not eligible for overtime pay.

Communicating With Gen Xers

An increasing percentage of the workforce and business managers are from this generation. Xers are the electronic generation that ushered in a plethora of products and software all aimed at being more productive: PCs, PDAs, cell phones, the Web, and so on. This is a generation of efficiency, immediacy, and directness. Everything has to do with information and how to get it. Consequently your communication style with a Gen Xer must be direct and contain the information he or she seeks (and not one bit more than is necessary). This group is prone to cut off a conversation or change the subject as soon as they have what they want or if the discussion is going nowhere. Their favorite word for bringing closure in those instances is "whatever." Traditionalists and Baby Boomers may be offended by that curtness, and even take it personally though that is not the Xer's intention.

This is a group that rejects the notion of long hours and the belief that this and hard work will get you ahead. They prefer to work smart, not hard, so their work/life balance is in alignment. Consequently, your approach to communicating and interviewing is to put forth ideas and suggestions dealing with productivity and working smart. Demonstrate to them how you will make their work easier.

Don't crowd a Gen Xer or try to control the interview. Be prepared to move quickly from one subject to another. Rather than dwell too long on a particular answer simply ask the person if the initial response is okay and understood. Also, be relaxed and informal as this generation views older ones as being stuffy and too intense. Work on being relaxed.

The difficulties for Baby Boomers or the Traditionalists who are extending their career beyond normal retirement or reentering the labor market, is that, like it or not, one most likely will be working for a Gen Xer. As discussed before, thoroughly understand what he or she is about, focus on his or her strengths and talents, and find areas of compatibility (usually factual elements, not style traits).

Communicating With Traditionalists

There are still many members of the Mature generation in the workforce, and it is quite possible you will be interviewing with such a person. More than likely, he or she will be at or beyond the age of 65 and in a senior leadership role (board member, owner, CEO, and so on). Because experience, to the Mature generation, is the best teacher, ask them about his or her own experiences and what he or she has learned about the business or the job for which you are applying. Use questions such as: "Based upon your experience with this job, what are the most important elements?", "And why?", and "At your level you certainly have a broad view of the business. What role does this position play in the overall picture?"

Because the Traditional generation is also about rules, structure, and organizational hierarchy, ask them about it. The information will tell you a lot about the work environment and expectations within which you will be operating. Ask a questions such as: "Everyone has his or her own way of structuring an organization, its process and people. Tell me about how you like to operate."

It is highly possible that the traditionalist with whom you interview will have been employed by the company for many years. Traditionalists do not switch jobs often. They are very loyal to their employer and like the security of that relationship. Consequently, tread lightly where your discussion involves change, radically new ideas (versus good suggestions), thoughts on reorganization, and so on. The individual may feel threatened with your presence in the organization, and pass you over or recommend you not be hired. Instead, talk about how you like to work with experienced people who can assess your ideas, give direction, and help implement. Similar advice goes for conversations with a Baby Boomer.

People of this generation are letter and memo writers. E-mail is a recently introduced communication tool and although many are adept at using and sending e-mails, most would prefer receiving their communications the old-fashioned way (in the form of a written letter or note).

Communicating With the Millenium Group

Even though this generation is just coming out of high school and college, it is possible that you could be working for or interviewing with a Millenium person. This is a very collaborative generation and, as a result, they may request to be part of the interview and selection process. They are very team-oriented and will be looking for similar work traits in you. They enjoy being involved and receiving instant feedback (this is the generation that loves to do instant messages on the PC and send text messages on cell phones). Provide short responses with compressed information and ask for their immediate feedback.

If you are a product of the Baby Boomer era or the Mature generation, interviewing with a Millenium should not be as difficult as you believe. You probably are hesitant because the person is young enough to be your daughter or son, yet that is why you will be successful! Think about your own children who are, or soon will be, adults. Not only are they prone to say things the way they are, but they will put feelings out there, too.

Although categorized as an optimistic group of people, they often feel stressed and very busy. They have also been described as very ambitious individuals, yet lack direction in their life. As the more mature and older person you can be of help to them in the workplace with your know-how and experience. Share, in an interview, how you can do so, but make sure it is in a warm, nonthreatening manner.

Communicating With Cross-Over Groups

These are individuals whose year of birth puts them at the end or beginning of a generation. Being on the edge of a generation, they may or may not exhibit the style normally characteristic of the era in which their birth date falls. One's behavior may be more akin to the other generation, or it may be a blend of the two. Be conscious of when you are with someone with "cross-over" potential. There are some overlapping traits of the Gen Xer's and Milleniums such as desire for work/life balance and being technologically savvy. The Baby Boomers and Mature generations have "hard work" in common and place high marks on respect and authority. There are less cross-over characteristics with the Baby Boomers and Gen-Xers.

It is also possible for individuals to totally embrace the traits of the generation that preceded them. Someone born late or in the middle of one generation span may behave similar to the earlier generation. For example, a young Gen Xer may act more similarly to his or her parent, who is from the Baby Boomer or Mature generation.

In general, when communicating and interviewing with a member of any generation, start with the assumption that he or she "rings true" to his or her era. Approach him or her on that basis unless his or her actions indicate otherwise. Again, as with the four behavioral styles (*D*, *I*, *S*, and *C*), use the information to enhance your communication of facts, achievements, and job interests. Adapting your speech and phrasing to the other person's style and generation is a way of assuring connectivity. As always, moderation is the keyword as you seek to adapt your style without sounding fake or insincere.

Chapter Worksheet

▸ From which generation are you? Is it descriptive of you? If not, are you of a "cross-over" age?

▸ What do you know about the individual(s) with whom you will be interviewing? Do you know his or her age? If not, do his or her behavior and communication style ring true of a particular generation? How can you learn more about the individual before going into the interview?

▸ Based upon your knowledge or assumptions about his or her generation, how should you focus your communications and interview? What might you have to do to adapt your style in order to maximize connectivity?

▸ If you have already met the person and you know his or her generation, how might you use that to your advantage in future conversations or communications?

CHAPTER 10

Tactics That Get You or Your Resume Through the Door

A Surefire Trick to Get Any Letter Opened and Read

Since the boom of mail-order, catalog shopping, and Internet retail, most of us have received packages, envelopes, and so on, from FedEx, U.S. Postal Service Priority Mail, or other large parcel carriers. How many times have you decided *not* to open one? Never, right. Everyone opens it immediately. They are dying to know what's inside that had to be sent so urgently. Here's how you can capitalize on human nature's basic desire for special treatment. If you have a target and you really want him or her to take a look at your information, send it with special handling. It is almost guaranteed that the recipient will open it and at least read the cover letter. As pointed out in earlier chapters, your message still has to be compelling and unique. If it isn't, the packet will end up in the "no interest" pile or, worse yet, in the trash.

Staying at "Top of Mind"

One of your objectives is to get in front of the hiring manager and stay there. Although he or she may not have a need for someone with your skill sets at the present time, chances are, he or she will. When he or she does, you want to be the first person he or she thinks of. That will get you an interview or a phone call at the minimum. Unfortunately, people have short memories. There are far more pressing matters for the hiring manager than job seekers they aren't currently in need of. For this reason, you need to keep reminding him or her, in an unobtrusive manner, that you are there. You want to let him or her know you are there, but don't want to become a pest. There are a number of ways you can do this:

> ▶ Periodic status updates. Write or e-mail the individual when you finished a key project at your company. Do the same when you receive an award or promotion, or begin or complete an advanced degree program. Similarly, alert the person to changes in your company (acquisitions, new sales and profit levels) and your involvement. The point is to keep your name in front of the person and your resume in his or her "talent" file.

> ▶ Send news clippings and business articles that are interesting or relevant to him or her and the company. These can include articles about his or her company, industry, hobbies, or just about anything (upcoming conferences, association meetings, networking contacts, and so on). Remember: The longer you stay on his or her radar screen, the better your chances of catching him or her at the right time...when he or she has a need for someone such as you.

> ▶ Articles or publicity about you. Whenever you are part of a PR release, local newspaper interview or article, trade or professional association

write-up, or even a human-interest article, send copies to these people. Better yet, make your own headlines by writing an article for a local paper or business magazine, a blog, an alumni newsletter, and so on. Another way to get your name in print media is to contact a local, regional, or national writer who pens newspaper stories or articles in your general discipline. These writers are constantly searching for sources to support and strengthen their articles. It also makes for a more interesting read when independent experts are quoted and add color to the article. One way to find these writers is to look through your local papers, business or professional journals, blogs, and newsletters and see who the staff writers are. Contact them and tell them, very briefly, who you are and what your area of expertise is, and volunteer as a source for future pieces. Don't be shy, as this saves them a lot of time finding a source when they are working feverishly to meet a deadline.

When All Else Fails…
the Office Delivery/Drop-Off

What if you have exhausted all means of reaching the decision-maker(s) for a position you seek? You have tried letters, e-mails, applied online, sent in your resume, and perhaps even received a "thanks, but no interest" response. You really believe that you are the right person for the job, but you can't seem to get his or her attention. You know that, if you could get in front of him or her, you could demonstrate your worth. You are at your wit's end and open to any ideas. Because you have nothing to lose at this stage you might consider some unique or even "off-the-wall" approaches to getting the person's attention.

What if you delivered a note and your resume with something nice for the hiring manager? It is an attention-getter and enables you to take advantage of what psychologists refer to as the *reciprocity principle*. This simply means that when you give someone something he or she feels the need to do something positive for you in return. Studies have shown that even when you give something of little or no value, the recipient feels the need to give you something. What you are hoping for, of course, is a call, interview, or referral. Again, you are trying to get a few minutes in front of the person or on the phone. A drop-off item should never be expensive, just thoughtful. Here are just a few of your options.

▸ Homemade preserves.
▸ Plants.
▸ A meal or a snack.
▸ Muffins or cupcakes.
▸ Coffee.
▸ Candles.
▸ Wine.
▸ A book.
▸ Fruit.

If you are hesitant about doing this just remember that you have nothing to lose. Your initial communication and resume obviously have not caught his or her attention. Perhaps it was read and decided there is not a fit. Your e-mail and voice mails have been ignored, or evoked a "no thanks" response. All attempts to talk directly with the recruiter or hiring manager have been nixed. You may even have received a rejection letter. It is not going anywhere unless you find a way to have a dialogue with the person. So try the drop-off technique.

Are you open to trying even more provocative means of getting the individuals attention? The following are examples of somewhat "off the wall" approaches. No one knows the odds of their success, but then nothing else has worked.

Consider these as methods of last resort. You can fill in the details.

 ▸ Contact lens solution with your own label that states, "I'm the clear solution."
 ▸ Paper-airplane resume with "I fly higher" written on the sides.
 ▸ Squash: "I'll help squash the competition."
 ▸ Thinking-cap resume.
 ▸ Peanuts: "I'm nuts about this job or your company."
 ▸ Soap: "I'll clean up."
 ▸ Light bulb: "I'll give you my brightest."
 ▸ Toy telephone with a note reading: "Call me."
 ▸ Raisins: "I'm raisin the bar."
 ▸ Shot glass: "Give me a shot."
 ▸ Cool pen: "I'll write new business."

Who knows, you may get a call. It may be positive, or a request to "cease and desist." Either way, you now have the person on the line—the rest is up to you. You might confess that it was a bit "silly," but "seriously," tell him or her you truly believe you are an excellent fit for the position, summarize why, and ask for an interview.

Chapter Worksheet

 ▸ What can you do to get your resume read?
 ▸ Are there individuals with whom you should be staying in touch? How might you find a reason to write or call the persons?
 ▸ What can you do to get through the door?
 ▸ Is there anything you can do, as a last resort, to gain the employer's attention?

CHAPTER 11

Success Factors and Additional Tips

Getting Ready to Create a Plan of Action

Seeking employment takes effort. It is rare that opportunities are handed out on a silver platter. For that reason, the key is to make a plan. The main focus of the plan is to decide what level of commitment you want to put into your search. This includes the number of potential employers you intend to call each day and what other activities you anticipate doing to achieve your goal. For some, it will include a plan to prevent yourself from getting discouraged throughout tougher parts of the search. For others, it will include a list of resources you intend to use in your search.

Building That Plan

The first step to any job-hunting campaign should be to develop a plan of action. Although this phase is important, remember that the action phase is where you will begin to generate leads. That being said, don't spend more than half a day developing a rough plan before moving on to the next stage. This plan isn't supposed to be perfect or ironclad. It simply identifies your goals and builds a rough roadmap to get you there.

The first part of the action plan is to decide how much time you are going to be able to allocate to your search. It is more important to be realistic and spend an amount of time in which you can be highly productive than to allocate more time and be less effective. Once you have budgeted your time, next create your goal for the number of contacts you plan to make daily. Be realistic in this goal. I recommend 40–60 daily contacts for the full-time job hunter. The last part of the plan is setting a goal for landing the job. A good rule of thumb is that it should take one month for every $20,000 in salary you are looking for. For example, a person who is seeking $40,000 yearly should be able to find employment in about two months. In setting your target compensation, a general rule is to seek 10–15 percent above your last salary in a strong market. Obviously, in a poor market, or if you plan to change industries or specialties, different rules apply. You may have to accept a lateral move or even a reduction in salary durring a lean job market.

Once you have created a plan of action, try not to deviate from it, and don't get overwhelmed if you fall short on any part. The most important thing is to keep going and continue to generate action; results will follow.

Finding Openings

This part of the job search takes creativity and perseverance. There are many different ways to find openings and get your name out there. Each has its own merits. Every individual has different skills that will make him or her more effective at some methods and less effective at others. If you haven't already done so, make sure that you are familiar with all of the techniques described in Chapter 1.

Finding the Right Recruiter

To help you along the way, I recommend that job-seekers work with reputable staffing firms that either specialize in the same industry as the job-seeker or are more general in nature. Staffing agency fees are paid by the client, not the applicant. Be wary of any agency that is looking to earn a fee from the applicant, as this is not considered to be an ethical practice within the staffing industry. Similarly, be cautious about granting an agency an exclusive, especially if it requires an inordinate amount of time in which to conduct its search. I find that it is advantageous for job-hunters to work with several firms simultaneously in order to cover as much ground as possible.

This can be one of the most efficient ways to land the right job. Specialists often focus either horizontally in one industry (for example, advertising agencies, publishers, law firms, and so on), or vertically by trade (for instance, graphics, information technology, accounting, light industrial, and so on). One of the best ways to find a recruiter who specializes in your niche is to look at job listings online. Look for positions (held by recruiters) that are either in your industry or in your trade. No matter how irrelevant these positions may seem, these recruiters probably specialize in your area of expertise. Although the jobs posted may not be appropriate for you, chances are they know of other openings. Also, new opportunities come across recruiters' desks every day.

Keep in mind that these recruiters get many resumes. It is important to stick out in their minds as much as possible. A telephone introduction is an excellent idea. If you can get a personal meeting it is even better. (Don't be discouraged if this type of meeting isn't possible at the present time.)

Each recruiter has his or her own way of working, and his or her own preferences. Be sure to ask how he or she would prefer you to send your resume. Some recruiters won't even look at a resume if it isn't sent electronically, and others only handle resumes that are mailed to them the old-fashioned way. Either way, you want to increase your chances of success with that recruiter, so be certain to follow his or her directions. It is also important to follow up with the recruiters you use to remain fresh in his or her mind. Every few weeks let them know of any new skills or relevant experience you may have added to your competencies.

Interview Protocol

Although there are different conventions in different industries, there are some interview protocols that are universal. For the most important ones, take a look at these guidelines.

Show up on Time

Many people understand that showing up late is not acceptable. If it is unavoidable, call ahead and hope for the best. Similarly, showing up early is not great either, as it may place an additional burden on the interviewer. The best thing to do is to be on time. I recommend arriving 20 minutes early and either waiting in the car or going for a walk until the agreed-upon time.

Dress for Success

Wearing a well-pressed, properly-fit, high-quality suit has such a strong impact when interviewing for any position. Do not try to get a less expensive suit than the best. If you buy a bargain suit for a few hundred dollars, I guarantee it will look as if you did just that. Similarly, if you buy the best and have it tailored perfectly, you will look very sharp, confident, and competent. Although it is a big investment, it is just that. It will last for years and give you the best chance to land the right job. It should pay for itself many times over by the time you need to finally retire it. With this kind of edge so easy to attain, it's inexcusable not to use it to your advantage.

The Handshake

A proper handshake that is firm, but not bone-crushing, can leave a potential employer with a very positive and lasting impression. If you are not certain of the quality of your handshake, have someone you respect review the procedure with you. Although this may sound rudimentary, it is surprising how few people have mastered the art of the handshake. A handshake should be firm and deliberate, and convey confidence.

Be Prepared

Make sure that you do adequate research on the company you will be interviewing with, have good questions (prepared with the help of Chapter 3) ready to ask the interviewer, and bring at least four copies of your resume, two pens, and a note pad. It is also a good idea to have copies of written references with you. This kind of third-party endorsement can make all the difference.

The Winning Attitude

Few attributes can be as attractive to hiring managers as the "right attitude." This usually means confidence, enthusiasm, desire, and flexibility. Showing genuine interest in the job and giving strong evidence that you have the skills necessary to perform the related duties will go a long way. This, paired with a positive mindset, can be all that it takes to land the right job.

Hard Work

This does not mean working more hours!!! What is essential to amplify your effectiveness is increasing your personal output. This can be achieved through increasing your commitment to succeeding, maintaining intensity during time dedicated to your search, and making sure that no moment is idly wasted.

This level of focus, wherein you utilize every moment of this time period to achieve maximum output, will result in increased energy, satisfaction, and results. You will feel good at the end of each day, just knowing that you put in your best effort, leaving you with no regrets or conflicting emotions that drain your personal energy level on a daily basis.

People are often concerned that hard work will lead to burnout. I assure you that this is not the case. Burnout is caused by lack of success, lack of focus, and inner conflicts that lead to low output. This, in turn, leaves the individual feeling over-worked and unproductive. If you work hard on good leads and stay highly focused, you will have success and avoid burnout. It is essential when you have just had a success not to rest and reward yourself, as this will lead to a lull in your activity pipeline and cause potentially a downward spiral. Instead of resting, use the high level of energy from your success to create more activity (leading to more success, and an upward spiral). Similarly, when you are in a lull or feeling burned out, the best and only remedy for this situation is to force yourself to work harder than before, including starting early and ending late to get back on the path of success.

The Closing

At the end of the interview, thank the interviewer, and ask how he or she would like you to follow up. Make sure that you are able to follow up in the agreed manner before agreeing to it, because this is a crucial part of the process. Even after a spectacular interview, poor follow-through on your part will likely turn off the most enthusiastic of employers.

After the Interview

Now with the interview successfully concluded, there are important steps to take after the interview.

After a company has granted an interview, it is important to follow up as soon as possible in two ways. The first way is to follow up in the manner you discussed at the end of the interview. Although this should be relatively straightforward, if you have trouble getting in touch with your contact, be persistent. Remember that you have little to lose (and everything to gain) by being persistent.

This kind of follow-up is unlikely to turn off a potential employer. Sometimes, usually for one of two reasons, hiring managers don't return calls right away. Often, companies hire during periods of substantial growth. Things get to be very hectic, and managers become less and less available as their workload increases. Things not seen as urgent are often put on the back burner. At that point, it's your job to put yourself back into the forefront. Unfortunately, time is against you. Every day that goes by, the manager is being exposed to new candidates. The way to combat this is through persistence. Coupled with this persistence, it may be necessary to create a sense of urgency.

We never want to mislead a potential employer, but in all fairness to you, it is urgent that he or she come to a quick decision. After all, it would not be fair for him or her to prevent you from pursuing other options, if he or she is not really interested. In such cases, it is important that the hiring manager understand that you are a very desirable candidate. To that end, it would be best that he or she understands that, although he or she is your first choice, you may have to decide to go in a different direction because you have other opportunities and need to make a decision.

If the manager isn't interested (the second possibility), this could be for any reason at all. It might have nothing to do with you or your qualifications. It could be a poor match in terms of corporate culture, or his or her needs could have changed substantially. Whatever the reason, don't get discouraged and, most of all, remain friendly and courteous. There may still be a possibility that he or she (or someone the manager knows) might have a different opening that is perfect for you.

Because you have already interviewed with the company, you have an increased chance of landing that hidden job.

The Thank-You Letter

The second follow-up tool is a well-written thank-you letter. Extending this courtesy can go further than many people think. It shows, as the fine suit does, a certain level of polish. It also demonstrates your level of interest and willingness to put in the extra effort necessary to make a good impression. A thank-you letter is a must for every interview. Be sure someone proofs your letter, as a spelling error could jeopardize the job offer.

Sample Thank-You Letter

John Fre
11 Belden Court
Hamilton, MA 01610

[Current date]

Ronald Hooper
United Calding, Inc.
1600 Stremple Blvd
Antile, MA 01557

Dear Mr. Hooper:

Thank you for taking the time to meet with me the other day. I thoroughly enjoyed our conversation. I was fascinated by your unique approach, and hope to learn more about it. After meeting with you, I believe the job that we discussed is the perfect opportunity for me, and I hope I demonstrated my ability to perform at or above your expectations. Enclosed, please find copies of my references as per your request.

Best regards,

John Fre

Compensation Negotiation

Once you get to the point at which it becomes apparent that both parties wish to work together, a fair compensation package needs to be agreed upon. In some cases, an employer may offer an excellent compensation package right off the bat. More frequently, there will need to be some discussion and negotiation before an agreement can be made.

There are many factors that will influence how the negotiation will proceed. In the negotiation, both parties have a need and the final potential outcome is directly related to perceived value of the final solution at hand. In a candidate-rich market, the hiring manager's fear of loss is diminished. Similarly, with entry-level candidates, the perceived value is lower. In such cases, candidates have little leverage and will often either accept what is offered or look elsewhere.

For candidates who are filling a vital role, or are in an industry or market in which demand greatly exceeds supply, a candidate may have more leverage in the negotiation process. Although this is an important part of the hiring chain of events, keep in mind that ultimately the opportunity to work with the right company can lead to great things. Although the compensation package is highly relevant today, the overall opportunity is the really important issue.

Also, I have included an article on the following pages, published in New England Human Resources Association's journal, that gives good guidance to those individuals who are about to be (or just have been) laid off, fired, or asked to resign.

"How to Handle Being Pink Slipped"
By Peter Lawrence Gray , CEO, Peter Gray Associates,
12/9/2002

Fears of downsizing and layoffs have become common in this ailing economy. In fact, layoffs have become so regular that it has become accepted as normal for many. The big question when the axe falls is who will be next. I get many calls from people seeking advice who faced the axe themselves.

One of the most important things to do is prepare yourself for the possibility of being laid off. While many companies announce the possibility of layoffs before implementing them, others don't. Whether companies do or don't announce layoffs, there are usually signs to look out for. A few signs include: a drastic reduction in use of temporary staff and consultants, lots of closed door meetings between human resources and managers, a noticeable change in managers' attitudes toward their teams, perks evaporating before your eyes. If layoffs occur in your company and you happen to be one of the people who are laid off, here are a few tips that may help out.

First, negotiate with your former employer. Some employers may agree to willing to accelerate your vesting period on stock options, provide outplacement assistance, pay for unused time off, or increase the originally proposed severance package.

Once you have negotiated a fair severance, it's time to create a job search strategy. While it's tempting to take time off, remember that job searches can take months.

Setting specific goals is essential. These goals should be divided into daily and weekly targets and set in order of their priority. While many people update their resume, others forget to draft a cover letter and sample thank you notes. After confirming your references, request a letter of recommendation from your former employer. This should put you in an excellent position to begin networking with potential employers and industry recruiters.

Begin networking by identifying sources that may be helpful in your search. While you may have contacts within other firms or friends and family members who can get you through the door, many job seekers choose to work with recruiters also to increase their coverage. Recruiters usually are industry specific in their approach. Contacting a recruiter in a different industry than yours will probably not be effective. One of the best ways to find recruiters in your industry is to look online. By searching on the major job posting boards for similar jobs to yours, you will quickly identify recruiters who specialize in your industry.

Contacting these recruiters and potential employers is the next step. If you choose to call them, make sure that your contact is brief and your points are concise. Hiring managers take numerous calls, and you want to stand out without wasting their time. Be flexible in your approach and if you are asked to interview, make sure to dress appropriately, show up exactly on time. [Arrive 10-15 minutes early and go for a walk around the block.] Always follow up with the thank you note expressing your interest the opportunity at hand and thanking the interviewer for their time. If an offer isn't made, don't get discouraged, it often takes several interviews with different companies to find the right match. To assist you in this process, I have listed below a few of books on this subject which can be very helpful.

Getting Fired. Sack, Steven Mitchell. Collingdale, PA: Diane Publishing Co, 1999.

When You Lose Your Job. Hakim, Cliff. San Francisco: Barrett-Koehler, 1993.

Laid Off & Loving It! Madsen, Paul David. Growmedia, 2001.

Peter Gray is the CEO of Peter Gray Associates.

Possible
Section Titles

Although you should never use more than four or five sections in your resume, here is a list of possible sections depending on what you are trying to emphasize:

Academic Achievements

Academic Achievements and Honors

Academic History

Academic Preparation

Activities, Honors, & Organizations

Athletic Involvement & Special Abilities

Athletic Involvements

Background and Interests

Career Objective

Certification, Certifications

Class-Related Volunteer Work

Coaching Experiences

Community-/Class-Related Experiences

Current Address
Education
Education and Related Experiences
Emphasis
Extracurricular Involvements
Hobbies/Interests
Job Objective
Languages
Learning and Teaching Experiences
Major, Majors
Memberships/Interests
Minor, Minors
Other Employment
Other Experiences
Permanent Address
Philosophy Capsule
Present Address
Professional Objective
Professional Summary
References
Related Experiences
Special Abilities
Special Projects
Summary of Experience
Teaching and Coaching Experiences
Teaching and Related Experiences
Teaching Competencies
Telephone and E-mail Contacts
Work and Related Experiences
Work Experiences

Action Verbs for High-Octane Communications

Some action words have more impact than others. Wherever possible use the word that best describes what you did. Never understate your work effort and achievements. Start your phrases with words such as the following: "I was responsible for...." Remember that an action verb should be used to get one's attention and then the rest is up to you to describe what you did, how it was done, why, with whom, for whom or what, and the resulting outcome(s). Your goal is to create action phrases (printed or spoken) that have high impact. The difference is similar to using regular gasoline in your auto versus high-octane fuel.

> **Action verb + Noun** (describing the product, service, task, thing, and so on) **+ How Done** (method, technique, tools) **+ Metric** (time, people, quantity, quality) **+ end result** (what it does for your job, your department, or company, or what it means in specific terms) **= High-Octane Communications**

The order of the statement or phrase can vary. It can be stated in two sentences if necessary. There are two rules, however, when crafting a high-impact statement. First, always begin with an action verb (for bullet statements in resumes and letters, otherwise, when spoken, begin with "I" and then the action verb). Second, show not only the action, but also the result or outcome. Here are some examples:

"Reorganized product branding in three months by using customer-preference survey data. Eliminated retailer confusion regarding features and benefits by reducing total number of SKUs (stock keeping units). Overall tooling and production costs dropped 22 percent."

"Guided call-center department personnel through difficult company downsizing by keeping open and constant communications with team. Customer satisfaction stayed at 93 percent."

"Recruited and trained operations team (30 people) for new distribution center in Northwest in 48 days. Unit at full-shipping capacity after two months. Resulted in 22 percent decrease in time from date of order to home deliver of product. Process involved fast tracking of applicants and use of assessment tools."

Accelerated	Assembled
Accomplished	Assigned
Achieved	Assimilated
Added	Assisted
Administered	Attained
Advised	Beat
Aggregated	Bolstered
Amplified	Built
Analyzed	Carved
Approved	Channeled
Arranged	Coached

Collected
Communicated
Compiled
Completed
Composed
Compressed
Conceived
Conducted
Consolidated
Constructed
Contacted
Controlled
Converted
Coordinated
Counseled
Created
Cultivated
Cut
Delegated
Delivered
Demonstrated
Designed
Determined
Developed
Devised
Directed
Dispatched
Distributed
Documented
Edited
Enlarged

Equipped
Established
Evaluated
Examined
Expanded
Financed
Formulated
Founded
Gained
Gathered
Generated
Grew
Grouped
Guided
Hired
Implemented
Improved
Improvised
Increased
Informed
Infiltrated
Initiated
Innovated
Inspected
Instituted
Instructed
Interviewed
Introduced
Invented
Invested
Investigated

Launched	Recommended
Learned	Recorded
Led	Recruited
Maintained	Redesigned
Managed	Reduced
Monitored	Reorganized
Motivated	Represented
Navigated	Researched
Negotiated	Restored
Neutralized	Reviewed
Orchestrated	Saved
Operated	Scheduled
Ordered	Serviced
Organized	Set
Originated	Simplified
Outsourced	Sold
Parsed	Solved
Performed	Sparked
Planned	Staffed
Prepared	Streamlined
Presented	Strengthened
Prioritized	Stressed
Processed	Structured
Produced	Studied
Profited	Succeeded
Programmed	Summarized
Promoted	Superseded
Proposed	Supervised
Provided	Systematized
Purchased	Taught
Raised	Tempered

Tested

Trained

Transformed

Transitioned

Translated

Unified

Upped

Utilized

Verified

Vetted

Widened

Withdrew

Won

Wrote

Yielded

Job-Hunting Resources

Job-Hunting Sites

- *6Figurejobs.com*: for higher-level positions.
- *Academic360.com*: jobs in education by state.
- *America's Job Bank* (*www.ajb.dni.us/*): state employment office listings by state.
- *CareerBuilder.com*: excellent general resource and job-hunting site.
- *Careershop.com*.
- *Careervoyages.gov*: Very interactive Website sponsored by the U.S. Department of Labor. Topics include information about various industries, what the "hot jobs" are in Connecticut and the United States, projected salaries for various positions, and so on.
- *CollegeBoard.com*: for recent college graduates.
- *ComputerJobs.com*: the name says it all.

- ▶ *Craigslist.com*: This is a general resource and job-hunting site that includes nice discussion groups. The big companies do post here, but it can be hard for these listings to lead to interviews.

- ▶ *Dice.com*: an excellent site for IT and technical jobs.

- ▶ Experience Works (*www.experienceworks.org*): for mature and disadvantaged workers.

- ▶ *Freeagent.com*: perfect for freelance professionals.

- ▶ *Hiremenow.com*: fast, effective, and affordable.

- ▶ Hospital Web (*adams.mgh.harvard.edu/hospitalwebusa.html*): list of hospitals by state.

- ▶ *HotJobs.com*: one of the top, general job boards.

- ▶ *JobDirect.com*: perfect for candidates right out of college.

- ▶ *Jobfind.com*: a general job-listing site.

- ▶ *Job-hunt.org*: Advice on how to use job sites; important do's and don'ts for online job searches; additional lists of job sites for specific careers.

- ▶ *JobOptions.com*: a general job-listing site.

- ▶ *Jobs.com*: a general job-listing site.

- ▶ *Jobtrak.com*: a general job-listing site.

- ▶ *Khake.com*: Lists career paths, educational background, and job descriptions for many careers not requiring four-year college degrees.

- ▶ Labor Unions in the United States. (*www.XPDNC.com*).

- ▶ *Monster.com*: a superb national job board.

- ▶ *Net-Temps.com*: specializes in temporary positions.

- ▶ *Newspapers.com*: newspapers and TV stations by city within state (or country).

- ▶ *Onestopcoach.org*: A portal to federally-funded sites that includes a job bank, skills assessment, and relocation and salary information. Very rich content and superb online guidance for use of the site!

- *RecruitersDirectory.com*: extensive collection of recruiters (more than 10,000 entries), searchable by location and/or by specialty.
- *Salary.com* and *Salaryexpert.com*: Both sites provide free estimates of salaries for hundreds of occupations—search by zip code, industry, and so on.
- *Simplyhired.com*: A clean, simple interface for searching jobs by keyword or zip code.
- *Theladder.com*: a general job-listing site with great advice.
- USA Jobs (*usajobs.gov*): More than 20,000 federal government job openings. Search by department, state, salary requirement, and job category/function (for example, accounting, postal service, and so on).

Directories of Recruiters:

- Kennedy Directory of Executive Recruiters (*www.kennedyinfo.com*)
- *Recruiterlink.com*
- Oya's Directory of Recruiters (*www.irecruit.com*)
- Recruiters Online Network (*www.recruitersonline.com*)
- Recruiters Directory (*www.recruitersdirectory.com*)
- *SearchFirm.com*

Resume Distribution Services

- *www.blastmyresume.com*
- *www.job.com*
- *www.ProgrammerBlaster.com*

- ▸ *www.recruitercontacts.com*
- ▸ *www.resumeblasters.com*
- ▸ *www.resumepath.com*
- ▸ *www.resumeviper.com*
- ▸ *www.resumezapper.com*
- ▸ *www.seemeresumes.com*
- ▸ *www.employment911.com*

Job Cross-Posting Aggregators

These sites let you post your resume and information simultaneously with several jobs sites.

- ▸ *www.postonce.com*
- ▸ *www.careerfile.com*
- ▸ *www.recruitersonline.com*

Business and Personal Competency Traits From A to Z

When interviewing, you should expect a barrage of questions regarding your competency levels (new politically correct word for job and personal skills). Interviewers will be evaluating you on these skills, either through direct questioning or by drawing conclusions from multiple observation points. In preparation for an interview jot down your answers to questions about these hard and soft skills. Give thought to the five or six of these that are your forte. Use them when asked "What are your strengths?" Pay attention to the competencies stated in the job description or candidate requirements put forth in the recruitment advertisement. Although we didn't particularly respond to a job ad because it specified "must be a team player," or "must have strong written and oral communication skills," we certainly should expect the subject(s) to come up during an interview in the form of questions or interviewer observations. Reflect upon the meaning of the following competencies, and to how you would describe yourself. Think of examples that illustrate your personal mastery of each competency. Think of them in terms of specific situations with specific, measurable outcomes.

An interviewer can approach a competency in many different ways. For example, the competency of "leadership" might be addressed as follows:

"Define the term 'leadership' for me."

"What are the traits of a good leader?"

"Describe your leadership style."

"Give me an example of an ineffective leader."

"Tell me about a time when you had to form a team." [has to do with leadership]

"Are you a good leader?" [Answer yes and follow up with a statement.]

"How would others describe your effectiveness as a leader?"

"Talk to me about leadership. What does it mean to you?"

Your task, ahead of an interview, is to review the job description, recruitment advertisement, and any other materials that might provide insight into the competencies that are critical for success in the job, and your own depth in those categories. Following are some typical competencies and their definitions. Your task is to develop phrases that accurately relay your traits in those areas. Be prepared to not only put forth a phrase, but also to back it up with examples. Your examples should be situational and reflect outcomes and, where possible, metrics.

Budgeting: The ability to identify, calculate, and track expenses associated with a project, department, business unit, or proposal.

Character: This has to do with your personal qualities, integrity, morality, ethics, and reputation.

Coaching: The act of instructing employees on their job skills, behavior and performance. The end result of coaching is to alter and improve one's performance and affect new behaviors.

Commitment: When one is dedicated to a cause, project, position, or action, he or she is committed. It deals with one's resolve to stay the course over time and complete what was started or promised.

Computer Skills: One's ability to work with a personal computer and associated software (such as word processing, spreadsheet, presentation, and e-mail programs) plus advanced software (such as database or industry/business specific software, project management tools, modeling and forecasting, and so on). For the individual whose profession is computers, networks, servers, software programming, hardware, and so on. it is important that you know your skill levels and years of experience in each of your competencies.

Consistency: By conforming to past practices (that is, doing things the same way), one is consistent. Consistency generates predictable outcomes.

Crisis Management: The ability to respond to a crisis situation and to manage or minimize the subsequent outcomes for employees, customers, and the company.

Customer-Relations Skills: One is effective with customers when issues are resolved in a timely, courteous, and mutually acceptable solution. Someone with excellent customer-relations skills is adept at handling diverse situations and personalities.

Detail Orientation: The manner in which one pays attention to details and accounts for any and all possibilities. It means making sure even the smallest items are accounted for.

Developing People: One responsibility of leaders, managers, and supervisors is to develop their people. This means identifying strengths, shortcomings, and potential, and creating an action plan for growth.

Diplomacy: The ability to deal in a tactful and skilled way with customers, employees, peers, and bosses. It involves reaching agreement (or having disagreements) without alienating the other person.

Education (developing self): Paying attention to one's own development and growth by participating in workshops, formal classroom training, advanced degrees, institute or association programs, and so on. Similarly, it involves identifying new areas of knowledge that are necessary to be effective in one's job, and securing training in the same.

Employee Relations: The ability to deal effectively with employees with an open, balanced mind. The knacks of being able to listen, respond, explain, and resolve issues with employees.

Energy: The effort, strength, and excitement exhibited when doing one's job.

Evaluating and Appraising Employees: Being objective and timely in providing feedback to employees. Having the ability to assess and communicate performance, discuss the findings, and generate improvement.

Forecasting Skills: The ability to take available information and past experiences and predict, with a degree of accuracy and certainty, the business outcome.

Goal-Setting: Identifying what must be accomplished and how it will be achieved. Setting objectives, and the action plans needed to accomplish them.

Incisiveness: Taking or making immediate, clear, and unambiguous actions or decisions.

Negotiation Skills: Reaching consensus or agreement with individuals, groups, or companies through bargaining and discussion. The ability to reach a win-win outcome where both party's needs and expectations are met.

Organization Knowledge: Understanding the company, organizational structure, key people, and processes by which it operates. Functions, mission, vision, and culture are also elements of this knowledge.

Patience: A personal quality of persevering in a situation with little or no complaining. This is needed to endure difficult and trying circumstances.

Persistence: Not giving up. Possessing *staying power*, and seeing an action or cause through to the way to the end.

Policies and Procedures: Possessing solid knowledge of company procedures, guidelines, and rules, as well as applying the same in an objective manner.

Product (or Service) Knowledge: Knowing your company's products and/or services, what they do, how they are used, how they are achieved, and so on.

Self-Confidence: Having faith in one's self. Believing in your abilities and experience.

Selling Skills: Having the knowledge and ability to apply skills (such as prospecting, presentations, negotiations, features and benefits, trial closes, and closing).

Sense of Urgency: Recognizing the need to take action, and to not delay such.

Sociability: Having the ability and personality to interact and mix with others in a pleasing, warm, and interested manner.

Steadiness: Not wavering or faltering in your work or response to a situation.

Strategic Thinking: Being able to see the big picture. The skill and art of having a vision, and being able to articulate this vision to others. Strategic thinking becomes strategic planning when tactical plans are developed and implemented to achieve the goals necessary to fulfill the vision.

Tact: Having sensitivity to the impact of actions and decisions on others. Knowing the right thing to do and say.

Teambuilding: Putting the right people together in the right environment to accomplish objectives. The ability to put together and develop a group that works as a team to achieve the desired results. Instilling teamwork traits in your people.

Versatility: Having talent or abilities in many areas. The ability to move about and adapt.

Vision: The trait or knack of seeing things before they happen. Taking today's information, trends, and technology, and identifying what will happen in the future.

Index

About
the Authors

Peter Lawrence Gray is the CEO of Peter Gray Associates, an executive search firm based in Stamford, Connecticut. Gray has assisted both privately held as well as Fortune 100 firms in industries including: financial, technology, manufacturing, advertising, media, human resources, consulting, publishing, and consumer products. Gray is also known through his monthly newspaper column that focuses on human resources and employment related issues. His articles and opinions are frequently published by local and national business journals.

John Carroll is a professional speaker, seminar leader, and organizational consultant residing in Fairfield, Connecticut. A former human resources executive with more than 25 years experience with several global companies, Carroll launched John Carroll International, LLC (*www.JohnCarrollInternational.com*) to help individuals and organizations uncover, effectively use, and develop their God- given talents. He has coached hundreds of individuals on advancing their careers and worked extensively as a recruiter. He is a sought-after speaker on reaching peak performance, leadership, recruiting, and human resource management matters as well as inspirational topics.

Praise for *Beyond the Resume*

"Easy and fun to read, *Beyond the Resume* is an invaluable guide to anyone seeking a stronger position or an accelerated career."

—Bill Radin, President, Innovative Consulting, Inc.

"This book is a must for anyone entering the workforce or anyone who finds themselves in the midst of a career change. It is the perfect gift for the graduate. I will be recommending this book to clients and friends alike."

—Andi Busker, CEO,
Creative Staffing Systems/WTN Staffing

"The creation of the definitive guide to finding a job! Well Done!"

—Eric Seplowitz, VP of Operations,
Incentive Programs Unlimited

"Equips the reader with a proactive guide to develop and execute a successful job search.

—Linda R. Scharf, CPC, Founder and President,
Judlind Employment Services

"Captures the essence of searching for and finding your next job."

—Chris Russell, Founder, FairfieldCountyJobs.com

"This is THE resource...a must read and a must do!"

—Dan Jacobs, COO, Florida Micro, LLC

"As a job seeker, you'll want many resources at your disposal. It's a must-have for anyone serious about looking for a job."

—Ted Smith, Associate Director,
Access Financial Executive Search